The Deep Dark Web
the hidden world

Pierluigi Paganini & Richard Amores

PAGANINI/AMORES PUBLISHING

RHODE ISLAND , NAPLES, ITALY

First Edition

The Deep Dark Web - Copyright ©2012
paganini/amores publishing 212 providenc St West
Warwick, RI 02893 - 401-400-2932

ISBN-*9781480177598*

Publisher – Paganini – Amores
Our **e-book** can be found
http://www.smashwords.com/books/view/247146
For information on book distributors or translations, please contact
Publisher – Paganini – Amores

Paganini –Amores
212 Providence St
Rhode Island 02893
Phone 401-400-2932 – amores@yahoo.com
deepdarkweb.com – uscyberlabs.com – securityaffairs.co

Graphics Designer –
Gianni Motta was born in Naples in 1977. He is a creative with over ten years in the field of communication, graphic and web designer.
Currently he is in charge for Communication Manager in a cyber security firm.

Acknowledgement:

Richard Amores gAtO's list :– Gianni Motta –who has done
our artwork, Jason Jacobs & Jennifer Gold-Orlando for
gelping gAtO hunt in the dark for Tor answers, and of course
the loves of my life Nancy, Alexandra, Talon, Grayson,
Migdalia (maggie) and Josiah (joey) – just one victory and
were on our way

Pierluigi Paganini list:-Gianni Motta who has done an
outstanding artwork, Luca Scotto D'Antuono, Mohit Kumar ,
Anthony M.Freed and Colonel Bill Hagestad II who helped me
and encouraged my passion for cyber security, and of course
the reason of my life, my treasures
Rosanna, Alessandro and Alessia.
A special thanks to my Hero and friend, the incredible
Richard gATo ...
"Only those who dare may fly" ... Sepulveda

About the Author's

Pierluigi Paganini

I'm Master of Engineering and Chief Information Security Officer for Bit4ID, a company leader in solutions for Identity management, but I'm mainly a fan of the security with a great passion for writing. I consider myself a security evangelist, I strong believe that security is a shared responsibility and I profess every day awareness on cyber threats. It all started with the first game consoles, the Commodore and the ZX Spectrum were systems on which I learned as a child to develop and that I disassembled and mounted at will.

I'm security expert with over 20 years of experience in the field and the passion for hacking and a previous engage led me to be a Certified Ethical Hacker at EC Council in London. The passion for writing and a strong belief that security is founded on sharing and awareness led me to found the security blog "Security Affairs".

I started writing in sleepless nights due to my second child that kept me awake, I started for a joke from scratch and in 11 months has exceeded one million contacts with a growing trend.

One day I ran into a strange guy, Richard Amores, a man with a great skill in cyber security and we decide to approach together the Deep Web topic. We worked some moths making researches and trying to explore the abyss of the parallel networks. We have decided to write a book to share with the readers our incredible experience ... this is just our first trip, more adventures are coming.

Today I continue to write for some major publications in the security field such as Cyber War Zone, Infosec Island, Infocec Institute, The Hacker News and for many other Security magazines and journals.

Richard (gAtOmAlO) Amores

gATO is a modern high tech security lowlife -Richard Amores was born amidst the 1950's Cuban Revolution in the small town of Santiago de las Vegas. Fleeing Castro's reign, his family relocated to NYC where he was subsequently raised until his enlistment into the U.S Navy to serve on the USS Saratoga CVA 60. After discharge, Richard secured a job repairing punch card readers, learning about the before little-known object known as the computer. His interests led him to discovering things from Ethernet and arch net, to token rings, spark stations and s100. Deciding to niche his interests into software development, Richard began writing code for Lotus Notes. With Richard's help, Lotus Notes developed "email with a database that you could write software that moved about on the network and then into the web." His talent took him to far and distant lands around the world, working with fortune 100 companies such as IBM, American Express, and Bank of America to name a few. After dedicating much of his life to software and security, Richard, newly retired, became the owner of usCyberlabs.com, a security blog that catalyzed the idea of his new book co-written with Peirluigi. His passion for public security education is readily apparent as readers delve into the likes of "The Deep Dark Web".

Table of Contents

The Deep Dark Web – the hidden web

Foreword

"Deep Web", two words that evoke in the collective imaginary a mysterious place on the web, full of pitfalls, the representation of the hell in the network, but is it really so?

Every time we read about the Deep Web we discover a space full of crooks and cyber criminals, the hacker's paradise, where there are no rule, no law, because has no sense the concept of identity in the reign of Anonymity. But there is a further aspect of the hidden web, a direct consequence of the ability to operate in complete anonymity, it is considerable as the powerful vector of freedom of speech, an undisputed bastion for those who fight for freedom of expression.

This Book is to give a clear vision of "The Deep Dark Web" to the reader; it wants to represent the compass direction in a place with no boundaries and dimensions, where each service may hide a trap, where Governments and law enforcements have no dominance.

Due the huge quantity of information hidden in the deep web and to its nature in the last years is increased the level of interest of governments and intelligence agencies in the dark space, new special units have been formed to try to infiltrate it and in many cases to block access to its networks.

Many governments consider the deep web as an enemy to fight that gives to opportunity to inside dissidents to propose to the worldwide attention their voice, for this reason they are acquiring network appliances to monitor and control the cyber space blocking the access to the "networks of freedom" such as Tor network. It is happened in Syria, Iran, Ethiopia, and China where the governments want to deny their own people free access to information, to speak freely about their grievances and unite to tear down their walls of oppression.

The Deep Dark Web – the hidden web

In the last couple of years we have assisted to the diffusion of cyber weapon use, such as Stuxnet, Duqu & Flame, we have read about clamorous data breaches like HBGary case, we have registered the consecration of the hacktivism and of Anonymous group, all those phenomena had a great impact on the ordinary web, but it's just the surface of a space exterminated. Every event has it's corresponding in the deep web, in many case is in this place that it starts, grows and explodes.

The deep web is considered by many experts a parallel world, more close to ordinary reality than to the clear web, it is for example the space where nonviolent movements have promoted their ideas, consider for example the Arab Spring wind, a revolutionary
wave of demonstrations and protests occurring in the Arab world starting from December 2010.

The recent revolution in Egypt that ended the autocratic presidency of Hosni Mubarak was a modern example of successful nonviolent resistance organized using Social Media technologies. All this events have been persecuted by the oppressive regimes in the clear web, they censored website and infiltrated and manipulated social networks. Be social, be political active was a risk, that way activists have decided to drive the insurrections protected by anonymity granted by networks such as Tor. Tor tools have become rapidly diffused between bloggers, journalists and online activists to protect their identity and to practice free speech.

The book approaches the use of deep web under several perspectives, it include arguments such us cybercrime, hacktivism, intelligence, cyber warfare all with common denominator to adopt the anonymity to persevere their scopes. The book raises several questions regarding the legality of Anonymity and the implication of its distorted use, it provides a detailed guide to the environments and tools to hide the identity during the navigation, no matter if you are a criminal that is arranging your business, an hacktivism that is proposing its ideas or a government that is monitoring the hidden network and its connections.

During our researches we have found the proofs of interesting hypothesis related to the use of the network made by intelligence services to have a communication secure media that would piggy-back on the establish Internet, for example a branch of the U.S. Navy uses Tor for open source intelligence gathering, and one of its teams used Tor while deployed in the Middle East recently. Communication is just one aspect of Deep Web usage, we have discussed also of the monitoring implemented by private companies and governments.

We show to the reader that a proper use of anonymizer networks such as Tor could serve also for legitimate purpose, it's the case of a journalist that is able to file reports before governments agents censored his work or the case of an executive that visiting a foreign country (like China know to monitor foreigners Internet access) has the opportunity to securely connect to their corporate HQ data-center without being monitored and giving away IP (Intellectual Properties).

A free network is a meeting opportunity, a place where two cyber security specialists like Pierluigi & gAtO have decided to make public their knowledge on a so interesting topic, noting that many security experts and common people are demonstrating an increasing attention in the deep web.

Human beings are curious by nature, we are explorers for the genesis and we with our free intend to accompany the reader on an unusual trip, exploring the secret chambers of a place still mysterious to many.
The book is the result of intense work, comes from a long collaborations of the authors, but mainly feeds on an assiduous study of cyberspace described, infiltration of months spent in areas inaccessible to many.

We started as a joke, outlining a table of content and started to write about it noting day by day the arguments were increasing such as our interest.
We desire to share with the reader our emotions in a trip in the abyss of knowledge where all is possible and where readers can find realities never unimagined.

How many people know about cyber criminals and their ecosystem in the deep web?
How many have provided information on the financial systems behind the "dirty affairs"?
We read often about cybercrime ecosystem in the Deep Web and about the fear of financial institution of an auto managed currency (bitCoins) that is replacing fiat currencies all over the world during these unstable financial times, but who can explain to the reader these concepts of great actuality?

We have searched for these responses providing our vision on the arguments.

Dear reader, we know that you will find answers to many questions on a so fascinating topic, but many others will crowd your mind after reading ... we will be here for, to help you understand and overcome our same difficulties.

Introduction

What is the Deep Dark Web?

Let's start with official definition; The **Deep Web** (also called the **Deepnet**, the **Invisible Web**, the **Undernet** or the **hidden Web**) refers to Internet content that is not part of the Surface Web, which is index able by standard search engines.

The name evokes the reader's mind to an obscure portion of cyberspace, inaccessible for many aspects unexplored, that is in part true. The roles and the procedures valid for the ordinary web are in many cases altered. The words "obscure", "inaccessible", and "unexplored" aren't casual, the resources in the hidden web are not visible to the common search engines, are not directly be referenced and so not simple to localize, but the most important factor is that the network materialize the concept of anonymity.
In the last few years the world has seen the Arab Spring uprising, London protest and riots, China, Syria and Iranians dissidents fighting for their lives and of course the hacktivism movement. The one thing that they all have is common is they needed to have a private communication channel were anonymity is paramount to privacy and their safety.

The **Dark Web** refers to the ToR-Project .onion hidden network that resides on top of the Internet -(also called the **Deepnet**, the **Invisible Web**, the **Undernet** or the **hidden Dark Web**) - refers to Internet content or hidden services that is **not part** of the Surface Web, which is index able by standard search engines.

It has never been so simple to use this secure network, users installing the ToR .onion program are able to access the new obscure world of the Deep Web, what is considered the abyss of the clear web.

Tor client allows a person with a simple Internet connection to tunnel and encrypt the pipeline so data and privacy are insured.

This book will accompany the reader on an incredible journey into the darkness of a world still little known even to experts. The deep web is now a mine of information, a space where freedom of expression and anonymity find their consecration, but at same time it is an uncontrolled area really dangerous due the complete anarchy that characterizes it.
We will be focused on the ToR-Project .onion network, we call it the deep dark web because it has both components of the deep and dark and websites called hidden services.

So what are .onion web-sties?

When we are on the Internet (surface web- clear web) we have Google, Yahoo, Amazon and most of these have a .com, .org or .net extensions this is how, when you type uscyberlabs.com the Internet can find the site by looking at a DNS (Domain Name Services) and get the IP address of were that site is and connect to it. Now we must remember that the Internet has become a business tool and it is under constant surveillance, every single click that you make is stored, filed, cataloged and analyzed so business can help you find what you want and suggest new products and services for you to buy. They monitor you, for your now good as they say, so they can provide you with better services is the old established sales pitch.

Who and Why has promoted the Deep Web?

We all know that the web was a DARPA project designed to allow scientist to communicate if a nuclear attack happened and later released to the public and became the web that we all love and use every day. The ToR .onion network was design, implemented and deployed as a third-generation onion routine project funded by the Naval Research Laboratories (and DARPA) developed for the primary purpose of protecting government communications, but now it's also public and it's a worldwide service for everyone that is provided by volunteers who set up onion routers (OR) all over the world. It's not controlled by anyone or any government. The way it works is the packets of data rides on top (and thru) the Internet so nothing special is needed but a simple software provided by the ToR-Project to allow it to tunnel and encrypt it's entry, exit point and information that it carries and allows you to have privacy and anonymity.

Who uses this hidden network today?

Well normal people, the military, journalists, law enforcement, business executives, IT professionals and activists and whistleblowers, but we need to add criminals use it too. Normal people use it to protect privacy from unscrupulous marketers and identity thief's, they use it to protect their communications from irresponsible corporations, protect their children online and research sensitive topics. The military use it for field agents to do their jobs, to communicate with Command & Control (C2C) and intelligence gathering. Journalists use it to communicate with their bureau safely, Voice of America and Free Asia/Europe help Internet users in counties of repressive and surveillance regimes to obtain global perspective on controversial topics such as democracy, economy and religion. Law enforcement use it to surf questionable web site without leaving telltale tracks, also undercover agents use it for the same reasons. Anonymous tip lines can leave IP addresses that can be traced with geo-location as a result a tip line web site would encourage anonymity to their sources. Human rights Activists and whistleblowers use this network to keep safe and private, while Internet censorships such as the great China-Firewall allows their people to have un-supervised access to web sites. Business executives can check out their competition and see what the market see's without giving away any information and when they travel on business like to China it can prevent the Chinese from snooping on their business communication. And of course IT professionals can also use it to verify IP based firewall rules, to test out a problem by coming into their websites from different locations and to have access to blocked sites by their companies.

Of course any technology, from a pencil to cell-phone, anonymity can be used by good and evil so criminals have jumped on the bandwagon and have built some hidden services to sell gun, sex, drugs and anything that they can. This small element of the dark web has given it a bad reputation but think about it you can find all these on the clear Web like craigslist and eBay so criminals use anything they can. One thing about this network that works against the bad guy's is they can't use it for spam mail since the ToR-.onion networks majority blocks smtp in order to prevent anonymous email spamming.

Anonymity is recognized by US courts as a fundamental and important right. In fact, government's mandates anonymity in many cases themselves: police tip lines, adoptive services, and police officers identities. Let's talk about the bad guy for a bit so you can feel safer while using the ToR-.onion network:

Today even if you don't want to use the ToR-onion network software to access the hidden services you can use proxy's with a .tor2web extension and have access to some of these sites. Of course you are not as well protected but at least you don't leave to many breadcrumbs to allow them to track you down. The ToR-Project has made software so any PC whether Microsoft, Apple osX, Linux or Cell phone you can surf with total anonymity. You can boot up from a thumb drive like Tails and leave no trace that you even used the computer because nothing is written on the hard-drive. You can use Obfsproxy to circumvent censorship, but all this will not stop governments like Iran. Syria, Ethiopia and China from trying to block people from access to the network, why

because it allows freedom from surveillance and gives people the freedom to have privacy. People always say:;
"If you got nothing to hide, what are you worried about"
but when people are losing their lives just because they visit a website like some in Iran and Syria it can be the difference between life and death for you and your family. The Arab spring showed that in Libya Muhammad Khadafy -was defeated without an occupying army.

Why we need Anonymity & Privacy Online

Deep Web and censorship

We clarified the use of **anonymize networks** is not only related to criminal intents, they represent in fact a powerful instrument to elude **censorship** introduced by governments in critical areas of the planet. We have provided the examples of **Syria** and **Iran**, but the world is full of similar operations that introduce a detailed monitoring as part of a government cyber strategy.
Let's take as example the Tor network and the censorship filtering made by governments to avoid that compromising

news could be divulgated outside the country.

As descried **TOR** infrastructure uses SSL connection this means that in case of SSL filtering it is possible to block related traffic. It's already happened for example early this year when Iranian intelligence blocked SSL protocol on national networks, making impossible the use of TOR network and also bridged access to it. Similar censorships have had a dramatic impact for freedom of expression and on free circulation of the information, Iran was one of the countries where the usage of tor network is more intense due fierce persecution of the regime against dissidents.

As we seen the Tor community replied to the censorship with the development of a tool to avoid filtering actions to restore the access to the TOR network.

Technically the filtering is implemented using Deep Packet Inspection (DPI) algorithms to the discrimination of Internet traffic made on the protocol. The algorithms define the rules for traffic analysis based on the inspection both data part and header of each packet in transit for a specific control point.

Deep Packet Inspection enables advanced network management and security functions as well as Internet data mining, eavesdropping, and censorship, and it is largely used by every government with purposes of crime prevention and defense for cyber attacks, but it is also used to reduce the openness of the Internet.

The most advanced filtering tools are **provided** by western companies. They market to countries that apply censorship such as **China**, Iran and Syria. They make money over principles as any good capitalist corporation does. Dollars over Rights.

It is very interesting that some projects related the Tor network and to its final purpose, Internet freedom, the Tor developers Arturo Filasto and Jacob Appelbaum have released OONI-probe.

OONI is the Open Observatory for Network Interference and its aim is to collect high quality data using open methodologies, using Free and Open Source Software (FL/OSS) to share observations and data about the kind, methods and amount of surveillance and censorship in the world.

Similar projects have been promoted to defend human rights and the observation of the levels of surveillance, censorship, and networked discrimination.

Basically OONI project has developed an open-source software tool, installable on every PC connected to the network, to collect data to analyze network interferences.

Unlike other censorship tracking projects like HerdictWeb or the Open Net Initiative, OONI will allow anyone to run the testing application and share their results publicly.

The Deep Dark Web – the hidden web

Figure 1 - Herdict Monitoring Project

The most famous interferences discovered with the tool are the censorship by T-Mobile of its prepaid phones' browser and also by the Palestinian Authority to block opposition websites. In this Palestinian case the minister responsible for the censorship was forced to resign.

Figure 2 - 2OONI Report on Palestinian Censorship

One of the main sources of information regarding the **monitoring** and surveillance activities on Internet is represented by **OpenNet Initiative** project that collects global data on Internet filtering using technical and contextual tools. The project produces detailed report on Internet control made in every country of the world, distinguishing the type of control and also the filtering type (e.g. Selective filtering, Substantial filtering, Pervasive filtering).

Figure 3 - OpenNet Initiatives

As we have demonstrated the monitoring of internet is worldwide recognized as a primary goal for governments, internet users are seeing their freedom of expression constantly menaced by implementation of filtering mechanisms for different purposes, due this reason as we will see many organizations are promoting the development of tools to elude censorship mechanisms, obfsproxy is certainly one of the most important.

Obfsproxy tool

We have just introduced monitoring and filter operations to block traffic avoiding free Internet access; we have also discovered that in many cases the implementation of DPI system could interfere also with the **access** to Tor network. Tor community has developed a specific tool, **obfsproxy** that attempts to circumvent censorship, operating a tunneling of the Tor traffic between the client and the bridge servers. The communications between user's client and bridges are usually addressed by applications for traffic monitoring that are able to detect Tor traffic blocking it. The traffic is suitably disguised in order to circumvent the control activities, this is possible through encoding and decoding operated by the interlocutors of the communication. Obfstool tool supports multiple protocols for traffic transformation, called pluggable transports; for example, there might be a HTTP transport, which transforms Tor traffic to look like regular HTTP traffic. The Tor team praises the "obfs2" module that adds an encryption wrapper around Tor's traffic, using a handshake that has no recognizable byte patterns.

Figure 4 - obfsproxy communication schema

The Iranian censorship and opportunity to test the obfsproxy tool

On February 10, the Iranian Tor users were unable to access to Tor network because the government had begun blocking all SSL/TLS traffic. The regime is reportedly blocking HTTPS security protocol, and preventing the use of software residents use to bypass the state-run firewall. As result of the censorship operation all Google services such as Gmail were inaccessible and also any website that replies on https.

Tor was a collateral effect because it's network uses SSL communications between client and servers. Following some graphs that show the evidence of censorship applied by Iranian Government confirmed also by declarations made by high officials of the government of Teheran.

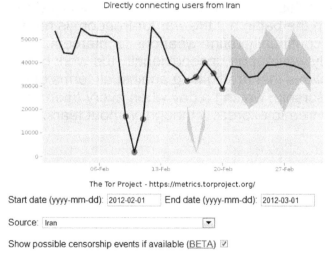

Figure 5 - Tor Metrics, Iranian user directly access Tor network

Tor Community prompted responded diffusing two "Tor Obfsproxy Browser Bundle" that was pointing a couple obfsproxy bridges. A group of brave volunteers tested the solution helping the Tor developers to tune the application. On February 13th the development team released a stable version with new versions of Vidalia, Tor, and Obfsproxy, It was a success as demonstrated by the following picture.

The development of censorship avoidance tools has the primary purpose to make difficult for the censors the definition of a pattern for the traffic filtering.
Of course is a first step in the direction of freedom, the bundle in fact included 14 preconfigured bridge addresses, if censors discover them they be could filtered. To avoid detection the developers have included in the new Vidalia release the possibility to manually configure the obfsproxy bridge addresses eliminating preconfigured addresses.

One of the main problems related to traffic analysis is the phenomena of false positives, the usage of monitoring system could block also legal traffic and a censorship avoidance tool could operate due to make difficult the filtering. In this optical have worked the Tor developers, they have won the battle but the war for freedom is hard and the censors continually refine weapons to intercept.
Obviously we support unconditionally the work of these organizations that are fighting against all forms of repression and censorship, waiting a day when every Internet users could be free to express it thought without fears.

The Deep Dark Web – the hidden web

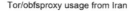

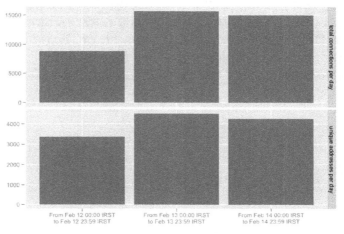

Figure 6 - obfsproxy in Iran test

The Chinese Tor Censorship

The most efficient censorship on Tor network has been applied by Chinese government with its "Great Firewall" project, in addition to blocking access to normal web, prevents thousands of potential Tor users from accessing the network. A paper on the method used by China to block Tor, reports that the government is able to intercept the communications to unpublished bridges stopping them in few minutes using a dynamic process.

http://www.cs.kau.se/philwint/pdf/torblock2012.pdf

In the past any censorship on Tor communications was made through IP blacklisting and HTTP header filtering, but the new-implemented mechanisms uses more sophisticated techniques able to block within only few minutes new bridges. After some researches it has been discovered the process used to block Tor traffic, following a typical scenario.

When a Tor user in China establishes a connection to a bridge or relay, deep packet inspection (DPI) device is able to detect the Tor protocol, activating a network scanning on random Chinese IP addresses in search of Tor bridges. If the scan finds a Tor bridge, the DPI tries to establish a connection on it, and if the connection is successful the

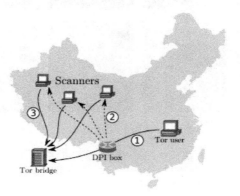

bridge is blocked.

It has been noted that active scanning is performed every 15 minutes; the appliances composing the Great Firewall of China launch several scanners trying to connect to the Tor bridges. Once a bridge is discovered Chinese scanners start a TLS connection, conduct a renegotiation and start building a Tor circuit, once the TLS connection was set up.
In case of connection successfully, the bridge is immediately blocked using its IP address and associated port.
The censorship applied by Chinese government starts making inaccessible web sites that host Tor application. The

Figure 7 - The structure of the Chinese Tor blocking infrastructure

filtering systems monitc
resetting all those conn............. .... p........ .... .g
"torproject.org".
So in order to avoid censorship it is possible to download Tor from mirrors that haven't the string "torproject.org" in the host name or simply using the HTTPS to access to the TOR resources.

Once obtained the Tor bundle a user tries to connect to the directory authorities and fetch the consensus containing the list of all public Tor relays, but almost all of the public relays are blocked from inside China.

It's clear that in similar scenario the user could try to access to the Tor network via Bridges, relays which are not listed in the public consensus, but unfortunately also related IP addresses are blocked by the censors.

Filtering system identifies Tor connections by searching as pattern the cipher list, unique to Tor, sent by Tor clients. The cipher list is part of the TLS client hello, sent after a TCP connection by the Tor user to the relay or bridge.

Tor filtering is probably only done at Chinese border blocking only outgoing traffic due the absence of relays inside China, Tor usage is exclusively made to connect to the outside world.

During the experiments made on the methods of censorship implemented by China it has been observed that once a Tor bridge has been blocked, it only remains blocked if Chinese scanners are able to continuously connect to the bridge. If they cannot, the block is removed.

The analysis of censorship implemented by China is concluded with the test of avoidance tool Obfsproxy, it has been discovered that all the hardcoded bridges addresses are blocked, meanwhile it is possible to reach a fresh relay established and not publicity declared.

What is the ToR Project

Overview

Inception

TorProject.org Anonymity Online Software – Protect your privacy. Defend yourself against network surveillance and traffic analysis.

Tor was originally designed, implemented, and deployed as a third-generation onion routing project of the U.S. Naval Research Laboratory. It was originally developed with the U.S. Navy in mind, for the primary purpose of protecting government communications. Today, it is used every day for a wide variety of purposes by normal people, the military, journalists, law enforcement officers, activists, and many others.

Overview

Tor is a network of virtual tunnels that allows people and groups to improve their privacy and security on the Internet. It also enables software developers to create new communication tools with built-in privacy features. Tor provides the foundation for a range of applications that allow organizations and individuals to share information over public networks without compromising their privacy. Individuals use Tor to keep websites from tracking them and their family members, or to connect to news sites, instant messaging services, or the like when these are blocked by their local Internet providers. Tor's hidden services let users publish web sites and other services without needing to reveal the location of the site. Individuals also use Tor for socially sensitive communication: chat rooms and web forums for rape and abuse survivors, or people with illnesses.

Journalists use Tor to communicate more safely with whistleblowers and dissidents. Non-governmental organizations (NGOs) use Tor to allow their workers to connect to their home website while they're in a foreign country, without notifying everybody nearby that they're working with that organization.

Groups such as Indy media recommend Tor for safeguarding their members' online privacy and security. Activist groups like the Electronic Frontier Foundation (EFF) recommend Tor as a mechanism for maintaining civil liberties online. Corporations use Tor as a safe way to conduct competitive analysis, and to protect sensitive procurement patterns from eavesdroppers. They also use it to replace traditional VPNs, which reveal the exact amount and timing of communication. Which locations have employees working late? Which locations have employees consulting job-hunting websites? Which research divisions are communicating with the company's patent lawyers?

A branch of the U.S. Navy uses Tor for open source intelligence gathering, and one of its teams used Tor while deployed in the Middle East recently. Law enforcement uses Tor for visiting or surveillance web sites without leaving government IP addresses in their web logs, and for security during sting operations.

The variety of people who use Tor is actually part of what makes it so secure. Tor hides you among the other users on the network, so the more populous and diverse the user base for Tor is, the more your anonymity will be protected.

Why we need Tor

Using Tor protects you against a common form of Internet surveillance known as "traffic analysis." Traffic analysis can be used to infer who is talking to whom over a public network. Knowing the source and destination of your Internet traffic allows others to track your behavior and interests. This can impact your checkbook if, for example, an e-commerce site uses price discrimination based on your country or institution of origin. It can even threaten your job and physical safety by revealing who and where you are. For example, if you're travelling abroad and you connect to your employer's computers to check or send mail, you can inadvertently reveal your national origin and professional affiliation to anyone observing the network, even if the connection is encrypted.

How does traffic analysis work? Internet data packets have two parts: a data payload and a header used for routing. The data payload is whatever is being sent, whether that's an email message, a web page, or an audio file. Even if you encrypt the data payload of your communications, traffic analysis still reveals a great deal about what you're doing and, possibly, what you're saying. That's because it focuses on the header, which discloses source, destination, size, timing, and so on.

A basic problem for the privacy minded is that the recipient of your communications can see that you sent it by looking at headers. So can authorized intermediaries like Internet service providers, and sometimes unauthorized intermediaries as well. A very simple form of traffic analysis might involve sitting somewhere between sender and recipient on the network, looking at headers.

But there are also more powerful kinds of traffic analysis. Some attackers spy on multiple parts of the Internet and use sophisticated statistical techniques to track the communications patterns of many different organizations and individuals. Encryption does not help against these attackers, since it only hides the content of Internet traffic, not the headers.

The solution: a distributed, anonymous network

Tor helps to reduce the risks of both simple and sophisticated traffic analysis by distributing your transactions over several places on the Internet, so no single point can link you to your destination. The idea is similar to using a twisty, hard-to-follow route in order to throw off somebody who is tailing you — and then periodically erasing your footprints. Instead of taking a direct route from source to destination, data packets on the Tor network take a random pathway through several relays that cover your tracks so no observer at any single point can tell where the data came from or where it's going.

To create a private network pathway with Tor, the user's software or client incrementally builds a circuit of encrypted connections through relays on the network. The circuit is extended one hop at a time, and each relay along the way knows only which relay gave it data and which relay it is giving data to. No individual relay ever knows the complete path that a data packet has taken. The client negotiates a separate set of encryption keys for each hop along the circuit to ensure that each hop can't trace these connections as they pass through.

Once a circuit has been established, many kinds of data can be exchanged and several different sorts of software applications can be deployed over the Tor network. Because each relay sees no more than one hop in the circuit, neither an eavesdropper nor a compromised relay can use traffic analysis to link the connection's source and destination. Tor only works for TCP streams and can be used by any application with SOCKS support.

For efficiency, the Tor software uses the same circuit for connections that happen within the same ten minutes or so. Later requests are given a new circuit, to keep people from linking your earlier actions to the new ones.

Deep Web Timeline And History
Dig up history of the Dark Net

So how do we do a timeline and find the history of torizens in the .onion network. You don't, you hope that the citizens of this new secret landscape will give volunteer information and find a place to document it. One torizens the administrator of MyHiddenBlog is one of the leaders in the .onion land he told me he was an administrator and wanted to develop services in Tor land to help the community and he has done a great job with little praise, recognition or money all on his own. He created a "The Abyss" a search engine in Tor, A bookmark site like delicious, a technical blog MyHiddenBlog and the

Onion land Museum this is where we found some timeline and history about the deep dark web. In onion land It's all about people helping the community to help themselves, so the information is very scares because you set up a web service in the onion to keep it secret, why document it unless you want the whole world to see it, but if they wonder by the Onion Land Museum maybe they will update this list and we will see a better picture of this world.. .
Since the beginning the .onion network has been a secret place were Google or Yahoo does not spider and search every site. While surfing I found this timeline in the OnionLand Museum –

http://kpvz7ki2v5agwt35.onion/wiki/index.php/Onionland%27 s_Museum

Welcome to Onion land's Museum. Here you will find links to articles about the OnionLand and it's torizens

- 2012
    - Operation DarkNet – Pedophilia forums were hacked by Hacker's BR Group, had their contents deleted passwords and broadcast around the world.
    - Reddit Tor opens for the new year 2011
    - In November-December, a rather nice amount of new non-CP image boards are created. Tor becomes more active as a few clear net communities hear about it.
- 2011
    - In August Dutch police target Hard Candy sites 4
    - On October 18th, Operation DarkNet begins. Hidden Wiki is dDoS and Freedom Hosting targeted.

- o Sometime in late 2011, Torbook opens its doors. This is an introduction to an anonymous social network on Tor; one of the first successful attempts of its kind. NOTE Torbook move to FreedomHosting
- 2010
  - o On October 22nd, Onionforum goes offline.
  - o In January, Jamon launches talk.masked.
- 2009
  - o In July Matt's services go down, probably for the last time.
  - o In January, ion creates a mirror of The Hidden Wiki, at that time hosted by Matt. (http://kpvz7ki2v5agwt35.onion/)
- 2008
  - o In October, Matt creates The Hidden Wiki (was this http://mihfrbaf562yakt2.onion/wiki/ ?)
  - o In August, Mixie's services launched.
  - o In July, Jamon re-launches masked. name.
  - o In July, Matt launches rock.onion talks.
- 2007
  - o In November, prof7bit releases the first version of TorChat. 1
  - o In July, Jamon launches core.onion talks.
  - o In June, new hidden wiki http://hy2644uxnz6zwt6c.onion/hidden/ starts up; in August it's down.
  - o In June 2007, long-running hidden wiki http://6sxoyfb3h2nvok2d.onion/ goes down.
- 2006
- 2005
  - o The anarchist news site Notes from the Underground goes offline.

- o In June, Legith creates Onionforum.
- o In June, Legoiv writes the first spider for hidden sites. 2
- o In May, Tor reaches 100 nodes. 3

MyHiddenBlog in OnionLand –
(http://utup22qsb6ebeejs.onion/ .onion site) -it is a great place for technical and security people to learn about the Deep Web's mechanics and inner workings.

We must understand that what we see in the deep web is limited only by you/us knowing where to look. In the Clear-Web (Internet)Google and Yahoo send out web-spiders to crawl the web and organize information about sites and their content, so if you are looking for the best place to eat sushi you can do a simple search and find not only a sushi bar but the location of the restaurant and which ones are the closer to your location. Let break this down so you can see how much data they collect about you. They know your geo-location and they know the geo-location of every place to eat near you, they know from what site you came from before you went to Google to search. They also know what device, make / model of your cell phone or computer that you used to do the search. Let's just say that when you travel on the information superhighway you carry a lot of information about yourself with every click.

Clear-Web Services – Dark-Hidden Services
How did you first find FaceBook or Twitter, someone told you about it a friend, fellow worker, also Google and Yahoo found it for you and feed you news about it.

So unless your friend or fellow worker tells you about a Deep-Web-Facebook, Twitter type-site in the deep-Web you will never know. Google and Yahoo do not index the onion network, these sites can exist and only a selected few will know, //---It's hidden ---// submit the site info to the "The Abyss" and/or "Touch" type Search engines so other find them if they search .--why so secret it's just the way of the deep-Web. By keeping it hidden they decide who know about it. The clear-Web is all about business it's built on the business model of information, information, and information. The deep-Web is about anonymity, not business.

The Government will tell you - only criminals use the Dark Tor network--// NO.
Example: Let's say you conducting a covert Para-military operation. You could keep a website in the deep-Web and update it and give battle plans but only your people would know where it is. Nobody can find it except your people. It's available 24/7 by any computer connected to the Internet and when you go in, nobody can find where you go, you can transmit data back and forth and your anonymity is secure. Do you think that the FBI, CIA and other don't use this technology. It's a military's communication system dream. **So good guys use the deep web too**. It's not only for criminal.

Difference between Tor network, .onion network, deepWeb, darkWeb and invisibleWeb

We have often been asked– what is the difference between the /ToR network- /.onion network- /Deep Web /Dark Web /Invisible Web – this is a simple question but it has many layers. Let's take a step back to get a better picture.

First we have the surface-web the Internet were Google, Yahoo, Facebook, Twitter take your information and sell it to the highest bidder to marketing people so they can sell you things you don't want or need but they make you buy the junk anyway.

Yes the surface web is where we live and do our banking, that's monitored too, research our medical problems and send our Twitter to the security community. Just behind the tweet there is curious story to tell, Twitter looks at our pattern and sells our information, the demonstrations is simple because going to Huffington Post to read stupid shit twitter follows us and monitors every article we read.

Difference between Tor network, .onion network, deepWeb, darkWeb and invisibleWeb
The ToR network: It's software that you get and install on your computer that allows freedom and privacy, confidential business activities and relationships without anyone knowing what your doing-
Install and you login to the .onion network but you can also use it to surf the surfaceWeb too.

When you are in the surfaceWeb you have -.com -.edu-.org in the .onion network you have sites that end with **.onion** the site names are kind of hard to read: (uscyberlabs is now in Tor -**otwxbdvje5ttplpv.onion**) this is the USCyberLabs web site in the Tor-.onion network it is part of the deepWeb and the darkWeb too.

Figure 8 - USCyberLabs web site in TOR

How so — it's on a need to know basis -and your not in the 1% club- you don't need to know my friend.

Figure 9 - USCyberLabs web site in TOR

The **Deep Web** (also called the **Deepnet**, the **Invisible Web**, the **Undernet** or the **hidden Web**) refers to World Wide Web content that is not part of the Surface Web, which is indexable by standard search engines. The deepWeb is the part of the web that Google, Yahoo and other cannot index so nobody knows where they are , except a few people. NASA for example has stored over 200 terabytes un-indexed databases and all kinds of reports that are part of the deep web.

The Deep Dark Web – the hidden web

Any un-index websites or web-services are part of the deep web, not the dark web that is only accessible by using the ToR-software.

USCyberLabs is in the .onion now it is part of the deepWeb/ but also part of the un-index deepWeb/ because it is not indexed nobody knows about it – it is hidden- unless I tell you about it. The USCyberLabs in the .onion is also part of the darkWeb because part of the dark web has an .onion after the website name.

But it's not part of the black-Market in the .onion network. SO now we have a ToR-network that can access the darkWeb and be invisible, untraceable so this is why crooks, and criminals use this network. Don't get me wrong the good guy's use the ToR network too. Why do you think that the

PhycOps is the deepWeb is for criminals the governments and business that want secure private communication are doing business on ToR while we stay away outside.

The fact of the matter is the more people use ToR-network to be safer the better it is for everyone, just go surf your normal sites, Facebook, Twitter it's ok your just safer. When there is normal ToR-traffic it becomes harder to see the dissidents that need ToR- network to save lives. Look at who donates to the ToR- project come on the -National Christian Foundation (2010-2012), do you still believe that this is not criminal network?

Hidden Services

What Are Tor Hidden Service?

Anonymity serves different interest for different user groups, to a private citizen it's privacy, and to a business it's a network security issue. A business needs to keep trade secrets or have IP (knowledge base data-centers), communicate with vendors securely and we all know that business need to keep an eye on their competition – the competition can check your stats using "site info" web site such as

http://**www.alexa.com**/siteinfo/uscyberlabs.com

and check on how your business is doing, what keywords you are using, demographics of users hitting your site——by the way in the Tor-.onion network a web site/service cannot be monitored unless you want it ...
How would a government use a ToR-network I'm asked all the time —

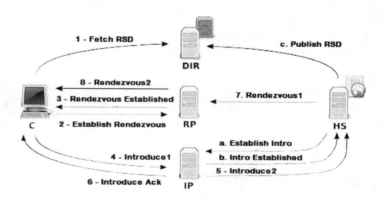

Figure 11 - Overview of hidden service establishment & access

If I was an (agent/business-person) state actor doing business in China (and other countries too) well I would use a ToR-.onion connection to keep my business private from a government that is known to snoop a bit on travelers to their country. The fact is governments need anonymity for their security -think about it "What does the CIA Google for?" Maybe they use ToR??? But this is about Hidden services right.

What is a hidden service in ToR-.onion network?
Simply put it's a web site/service, a place in the ToR network were we have a service like:
- Search Engine
- Directories
- web / pop3 email
- PM Private Messages
- Drop Box's
- Remailer
- Bulletin Boards BBS
- Image Boards
- Currency Exchange
- Blog

Figure 12 -rendezvous POINT not at my server/ my IP –No geo-location

- E-Commerce
- Social Networks
- Micro-Blog -

Hidden Services are called hidden, because your website's IP in ToR is hidden- **they cannot see the IP of your server — they can't track you- if they can't find you how are they going to hack you????**
Sorry I had to say that -((more about that later)).

Now how do I keep this secret (my IP) and let you the user use my services. In the normal web if you are in uscyberlabs.com you are on my site,— my server -you can do a whois and get my IP and geo-location— then you can attack my website with DDoS and other IP attack vectors, you also get my location so you can physically find me- my server/my website – maybe go dumpster diving in the trash and get my company secrets.

Well in the ToR-.onion network you the client ask the business website if they can use the websites service / then decide and start a handshake to a rendezvous POINT to meet —we meet at an OR ((onion relay))-a rendezvous POINT) not at my server/ my IP — so your never ever on the business site/server when you are in OnionLand, you **can't do a >whois** and get my IP because we meet at an OR – a rendezvous POINT, you **cannot find my geo-location**…

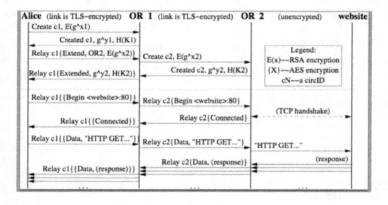

We have all heard of the killings of Iranians and Syrian rebels being in today's news, when an Iranian rebel is fighting for his and his family's life if they (the government) finds his IP or the IP of the website he visited // they will hunt that person down and the Iranian police/government will kill the whole family sometimes. So keeping an IP from someone is not an evil act it is an act of privacy for safety on both sides the client and the business.

This is one of the best examples of the good that the hidden services do.

Figure 11 - Now let's focus on R2 OR the yellow key. That's the spot where you (your company's hidden website) and

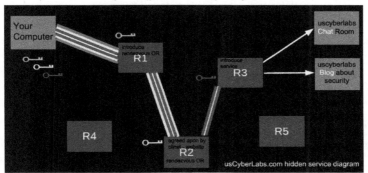

your client meet — I know it's a sneaky way of doing business but once again if they can't get to your IP at least that is one attack vector that can't be used to hack you or DDoS you.

OK they can still hack you but it's software then like xss, SQL-Injection. How it's all done – the magic —the technical thi**Figure 13 - Hidden service diagram**

the client /hidden web/service protocol.

Figure 14 - Handshake protocol

Event's goes something like this –
ESTABLISH RENDEZVOUS cell
INTRODUCE1
INTRODUCE2 cell
INTRODUCE ACK cell.
INTRODUCE2 cell
RENDEZVOUS1 cell

sends a RENDEZVOUS2 cell Chat
sends a RENDEZVOUS2 cell Blog
RENDEZVOUS *ESTABLISHED* cell

More Geek network kind stuff:

- Jun 03 20:50:02.100 [notice] Tor 0.2.1.0-alpha-dev (r14739) **opening new log file**.
- Jun 03 20:50:11.151 [notice] We now have enough directory information to build circuits.
- Jun 03 20:50:12.697 [info] **rend_services_introduce**(): Giving up on sabotage as intro point for stuptdu2qait65zm.
- Jun 03 20:50:18.633 [info] **rend_service_intro_established** (): Received INTRO_ESTABLISHED cell on circuit 1560 for service stuptdu2qait65zm
- Jun 03 20:51:18.997 [info] **upload_service_descriptor**(): Sending publish request for hidden service stuptdu2qait65zm
- Jun 03 20:51:22.878 [info] **connection_dir_client_reached_eof**(): Uploaded rendezvous descriptor (status 200 ("Service descriptor stored"))

How can these hidden services be attacked?

It all the same as in the surface web you find the software the hidden service is using /// let's say Worpress (or flatPress) if they use an old version with vulnerabilities then, that site can be hacked by traditional hacking attack vectors. Here are some technologies used in the ToR-.onion network:

TorStatusNet – *http://lotjbov3gzzf23hc.onion/* is a micro blogging service. It runs the StatusNet micro blogging software, version 0.9.9, available under the GNU Affero General Public License.

FlatPress is a blogging engine like -Worpress blog
http://flatpress.org/home/   – *http://utup22qsb6ebeejs.onion/*
-

Snapp BBS works fine in OnionLand -
http://4eiruntyxxbgfv7o.onion/ -
PHP BBS – *http://65bgvta7yos3sce5.onion/*

Nginx is a free, open-source, high-performance HTTP
server and reverse proxy, as well as an IMAP/POP3 proxy
server. – *http://ay5kwknh6znfmcbb.onion/torbook/*

Anyway I hope this open up the mystery of a hidden service
in ToR – it's just a website, you go to a rendezvous point and
do your business — your IP and the business IP are totally
secure. No digital breadcrumbs.

How to Use ToR-.onion Network

How To The Deep Web

Friends asked me, how do I go into the deep web safely?
We wrote this for that person I hope it help others:
I understand I was scared to go into the .onion myself but
have found that it has a wealth of information yes about the
good the bad and the ugly. For a security researcher It's a
gold mine to gather intelligence.

First step Tools:

Figure 15 - Deep Web representation

I suggest a Mac or Linux but even a windows VM box will
work. I don't use my windows machine because I have found
that it leaks too much information and I want to be silent
and observe and not be noticed.

If you really want to shield yourself go thru a **VPN first**.
Personally you don't need this unless your going into attack
mode then you want to be really shielded.
Next grab your Tor-Software to get into the game there are a
few styles to choose on how private you really need to be

https://www.torproject.org/

You can use **Tails which is a Ram Drive** to boot from any machine this does not leave a trace on your computer and I am sure that smart bad guy's use this, but I use – the basic Vidalia-Aurora Firefox bundle for my OsX Box-

https://www.torproject.org/download/download-easy.html.en

because I want the logs of my adventures for research. Once the Tor Bundle is installed it comes with its own Firefox… Use their version. Why? Because the regular version of Firefox has plug-in that if not proper configured could leaks data related to your host, but I said I want to be silent. If you want to have an idea on how much data could be obtained from you browser well check it oh the following web site

http://ip-check.info

Warning: *if you do find a say PDF or a DOC file click on it – it will ask you if you want to launch Acrobat say yes, then only SAVE the FILE- Do not open it right in the browser like you would in the clear-Web. Once again information leaks. Save the file and open it separately I know I'm paranoid but I like to be very safe.*

Once Vidalia starts it will also launch the (ToR) Firefox browser will open and I would suggest go to:
Tor Check <**http://torcheck.xenobite.eu/**
this will give you your **new IP** and user info:

Warning: always use SSL the bundle gives you that choice. I double check myself all the time on my site: In my site I bounce back your IP address so I check what my site tells me with what Tor tells me- trust but verify –
   http://uscyberlabs.com/blog/2012/02/05/recon-deep-web/

you will see below the spinning world your user information like your IP address check you will see that your IP in the clear web is different from the IP in the Deep-Web. I gave

you that page from my site since I use it all the time I have lots of ToR sites on this page.
Cleaned Hidden Wiki should be a good starting point for your adventures:

http://7jguhsfwruviatqe.onion

Figure 16 - The Hidden Wiki

This should get you started inside the .onion safely. Inside you will find that it is slow like the old day (modem slow) ha - ha

Tor hides communication patterns by relaying data through volunteer servers

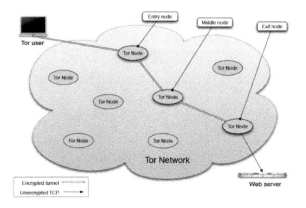

Diagram: Robert Watson

Warning: Some caution **CP= child porn — PD = pedophile** so be careful it's these sick shit and these are some of the scum I would like to fuck-up but that's another conversation. Lot's of places have a login first – register as a throwaway name and password unless you want an ID inside the .onion on that site. On every site you can register as a different user name so keep a log if you want to save your usernames for later…

The Deep Dark Web – the hidden web

ToR is slow and time consuming but there is lots inside for intelligence, the (ToR-Firefox) browser in Vidalia will work on the .onion web as well as the clearWeb. So use your Tor session and go to Yahoo and Google but guess what they don't know who you are – That's the ways I like it –aha – aha--I hope this helps…

Tor Products

Software & Services
The Tor community of software and services aims to make your Internet experience safer and better.

Torbutton
Torbutton is integrated into Tor Browser. Torbutton disables many types of active content and threats to your privacy when using a web browser.

Tor Browser Bundle
The Tor Browser Bundle contains everything you need to safely browse the Internet. This package requires no installation. Just extract it and run.

Vidalia
Vidalia is a graphical Tor controller. It allows you to see where your connections are in the world and configure Tor without getting into configuration files and code.

Arm
Arm is a terminal status monitor for Tor, intended for command-line aficionados and ssh connections. This functions much like top does for system usage, providing real time information on Tor's resource utilization and state.

Orbot
Tor community in collaboration with The Guardian Project, is developing Tor on the Google Android mobile operating system. A related application is Orlib; a library for use by any Android application to route Internet traffic through Orbot/Tor.

Tails
The Amnesic Incognito Live System is a live CD/USB distribution preconfigured so that everything is safely routed through Tor and leaves no trace on the local system.

Onionoo
Web-based protocol to learn about currently running Tor relays and bridges.

Metrics Portal
Analytics for the Tor network, including graphs of its available bandwidth and estimated user base. This is a great resource for researchers interested in detailed statistics about Tor.

Tor Cloud
The Tor Cloud project gives you a user-friendly way of deploying bridges to help users access an uncensored Internet via the Amazon EC2 cloud. By setting up a bridge, you donate bandwidth to the Tor network and help improve the safety and speed at which users can access the Internet. Get started with Tor Cloud.

Obfsproxy
Obfsproxy is a pluggable transports proxy written in C. It shapes Tor traffic, making it harder for censors to detect and block the Tor protocol.

Shadow
Shadow is a discrete-event network simulator that runs the real Tor software as a plug-in. Shadow is open-source software that enables accurate, efficient, controlled, and repeatable Tor experimentation.

Tor2web
Tor2web allows Internet users to browse websites running in Tor hidden services. It trades user anonymity for usability by allowing anonymous content to be distributed to non-anonymous users.

Who Uses the Deep Dark Web

Why People Use Tor-.onion network

We Live In A Cyber Surveillance Planet

You must be conscious that our OS is spying on us, every operation made is tracked and maintained in its components. Applications and browser (http://ip-check.info Check it out) Cookies, Extensions, Shockwave/Flash, Java, QuickTime, PDF and DOC, XLS, PPT … any time you open a document you leak information, you leave a digital bread crumb that major companies and governments can collect and sell on the open market and you have no say so it's your information.
They scare you by telling that only the criminals use the ToR network, in the reality they cannot collect information about you in the Tor-network, you are invisible to them and they don't like it when you play their game by your rules not theirs.

Silent information is being collected about us, this is the cyber surveillance World, cameras are everywhere but you have nothing to worry about from these devices because your cell phone is your worse enemy, it carries more personal information about you than you think have, in this way the businesses, politicians and law enforcement knows everything about your cyber-life ... and not only also you privacy in real life began an utopian dream. Just take a picture with your iPhone, the geo-location information and other data will be part of the metadata that is in-bedded in the picture, that's the way they caught the hacker w0rmer - Teamp0is0n group- he took a picture of his girlfriends boobies … She lived in Australia and they traced it back to Texas and got him…

FBI led to Anonymous hacker after his girlfriend ...
http://www.dailymail.co.uk/news/article-2129257/Higinio-O-
Ochoa-III-FBI-led-Anonymous-hacker-girlfriend-posts-
picture-breasts-online.html

Apr 13, 2012 – The **picture** shows a woman from the neck
down with a sign attached to her stomach, reading: 'PwNd
by **w0rmer**& CabinCr3w

In order to control us (the sheep and dogs & pigs) the
political in their essence of powers that we give them, seek
to extend the ability of law enforcement agencies to have
access to all Internet traffic data, a power that they largely
already have when it came to conventional
telecommunications, or email services.
But they want more and more. Everything that you have
typed as a message: the identity and time of your Facebook
chats, your Facebook likes, your Twitter feeds and mentions
too, the log your ISP keeps of the visits to all web-pages, the
clicks on an on-line polls, the location data of your phone
calls and access to on-line location services. The times and
places you were in the same chat room with your friends,
your on-line friends, etc. Do you know where you were last
Tuesday at 9:37 PM your ISP knows, Google knows, Yahoo
knows in fact everyone knows but you.
How about that kinky sex toy you bought from Amazon -for
yourself – you want mom to know this or the wife, boyfriend
or anyone for that fact, well they know....fact everyone
knows but you

Basically it's like having a cyber policeman following you
around 24h a day / 7 days a week, and making notes about
where you have been, what you have looked at, who you are
talking to, what you are doing, where you are sleeping (and
with whom), everything you bought, every political and trade
union meeting you went to, ... and they know your GPS
location and track you across central park too...– Traffic data
provides an X-ray of your whole cyber/real life, and the laws

suggests law enforcement and the intelligence services should have this information without any judicial oversight (only political review or police oversight).
That is why the ToR network comes at a time like this when all this is happening.

Here is a recent example of cyber covert war: -These are some of the covert-cyber-Ops that our government is doing. They use ToR network so the enemy does not see a .gov or .mil address, in the matrix you could be from Germany to China your information is confidential and you can proceed with your hacking at the enemies website and they will never know it's you.

How the State Department could of uses the ToR network

May 24, 2012 – US Secretary of State Hilary Clinton Reveals Cyber-Warfare Tactic's Against Al-Qaida:
Mrs. Clinton said the hacking was conducted by the Center for Strategic Counterterrorism Communications, based at the State Department, with expertise drawn from the military and the intelligence community. The State Department's activities are part of online efforts to stem the spread of radical Islamist ideology that stretch back at least a decade. The US Central Command had a team that monitors blogs and forums, targeting those that are moderate in tone and engaging with users, said Major David Nevers, former chief of the team.

"We try to concentrate our energy and efforts … [on] those who haven't been radicalized. The idea is to go where the conversation is taking place, using … extremist commentary or propaganda as a jumping-off point to people who are listening in."

Evan Kohlmann, a terrorism consultant who tracks jihadist websites, said the tactic could harm al-Qaeda's image among potential recruits but questioned its effectiveness on the ground.

"If you're already living in Yemen and in a tribal area, you probably don't need to go to a website to join al-Qaeda," he said.

Read more: http://www.smh.com.au/it-pro/security-it/us-hackers-take-cyber-war-to-alqaeda-sites-20120524-1z7rs.html#ixzz1w7P5y7S6

This was a lame hack in my humble opinion-- We don't need a total surveillance state- we already have one and they are monitoring us, and we are under cyber surveillance at all times. So escape and use the ToR network and be a little more secure, more private and safe.
When the Bilderberg group or the Skull and Cross or other groups of political/monetary influence meet their number one fear is that the mass now have a way for total anonymity. They (dogs) want to know what the sheep are doing, the need to herd the sheep is ingrained in their dna- to rule us- to protect us-.

This "**ruling class" thinks'** that they can **scare us into not using the ToR network**, telling us it's only the criminals that use the ToR Network. The cyber surveillance world we live in is fracturing, and they want total information control about US, but not on them———— *join us in the .onion network and be free from surveillance— gAtO oUt.*

Why Normal people use Tor

To protect our privacy from unscrupulous marketers and identity thieves. Internet Service Providers (ISPs) <u>sell your Internet browsing records</u> to marketers or anyone else willing to pay for it.

ISPs typically say that they anonymize the data by not providing personally identifiable information, but <u>this has been proven incorrect</u>. A full record of every site you visit, the text of every search you perform, and potentially userId and even password information can still be part of this data. In addition to your ISP, the websites (<u>and search engines</u>) your visit have their own logs, containing the same or more information.

They protect their communications from irresponsible corporations. All over the Internet, Tor is being recommended to people newly concerned about their privacy in the face of increasing breaches and betrayals of private data.

From <u>lost backup tapes</u>, to <u>giving away the data to researchers</u>, your data is often not well protected by those you are supposed to trust to keep it safe.

They protect their children online. You've told your kids they shouldn't share personally identifying information online, but they may be sharing their location simply by not concealing their IP address. Increasingly, IP addresses can be <u>literally mapped to a city or even street location</u>, and can <u>reveal other information</u> about how you are connecting to the Internet. In the United States, the government is pushing to make this mapping increasingly precise.

They research sensitive topics. There's a wealth of information available online. But perhaps in your country, access to information on AIDS, birth control, <u>Tibetan culture</u>, or world religions is behind a national firewall.

Why Militaries use Tor

Field agents: It is not difficult for insurgents to monitor Internet traffic and discover all the hotels and other locations from which people are connecting to known military servers. Military field agents deployed away from home use Tor to mask the sites they are visiting, protecting military interests and operations, as well as protecting themselves from physical harm.

Hidden services: When the Internet was designed by DARPA, its primary purpose was to be able to facilitate distributed, robust communications in case of local strikes. However, some functions must be centralized, such as command and control sites. It's the nature of the Internet protocols to reveal the geographic location of any server that is reachable online. Tor's hidden services capacity allows military command and control to be physically secured from discovery and takedown.

Intelligence gathering: Military personnel need to use electronic resources run and monitored by insurgents. They do not want the web server logs on an insurgent website to record a military address, thereby revealing the surveillance.

Why Journalists and their audience use Tor

Reporters without Borders tracks Internet prisoners of conscience and jailed or harmed journalists all over the world. They advise journalists, sources, bloggers, and dissidents to use Tor to ensure their privacy and safety.

The US International Broadcasting Bureau (Voice of America/Radio Free Europe/Radio Free Asia) supports Tor development to help Internet users in countries without safe access to free media. Tor preserves the ability of persons behind national firewalls or under the surveillance of repressive regimes to obtain a global perspective on controversial topics including democracy, economics and religion.

Citizen journalists in China use Tor to write about local events to encourage social change and political reform.

Citizens and journalists in Internet black holes use Tor to research state propaganda and opposing viewpoints, to file

stories with non-State controlled media, and to avoid risking the personal consequences of intellectual curiosity.
Law enforcement officers use Tor

Online surveillance: Tor allows officials to surf questionable web sites and services without leaving telltale tracks. If the system administrator of an illegal gambling site, for example, were to see multiple connections from government or law enforcement IP addresses in usage logs, investigations may be hampered.
Sting operations: Similarly, anonymity allows law officers to engage in online "undercover " operations. Regardless of how good an undercover officer's "street cred" may be, if the communications include IP ranges from police addresses, the cover is blown.
Truly anonymous tip lines: While online anonymous tip lines are popular, without anonymity software, they are far less useful. Sophisticated sources understand that although a name or email address is not attached to information, server logs can identify them very quickly. As a result, tip line web sites that do not encourage anonymity are limiting the sources of their tips.

Why Activists & Whistleblowers use Tor

Human rights activists use Tor to anonymously report abuses from danger zones. Internationally, labor rights workers use Tor and other forms of online and offline anonymity to organize workers in accordance with the Universal Declaration of Human Rights. Even though they are within the law, it does not mean they are safe. Tor provides the ability to avoid persecution while still raising a voice.
When groups such as the Friends Service Committee and environmental groups are increasingly falling under surveillance in the United States under laws meant to protect against terrorism, many peaceful agents of change rely on Tor for basic privacy during legitimate activities.

Human Rights Watch recommends Tor in their report, " Race to the Bottom: Corporate Complicity in Chinese Internet Censorship." The study co-author interviewed Roger Dingledine, Tor project leader, on Tor use. They cover Tor in the section on how to breach the "Great Firewall of China," and recommend that human rights workers throughout the globe use Tor for "secure browsing and communications." Tor has consulted with and volunteered help to Amnesty International's past corporate responsibility campaign. See also their 2006 full report on China Internet issues.

Global Voices recommends Tor, especially for anonymous blogging, throughout their web site.

In the US, the Supreme Court recently stripped legal protections from government whistleblowers. But whistleblowers working for governmental transparency or corporate accountability can use Tor to seek justice without personal repercussions.

A contact of ours who works with a public health nonprofit in Africa reports that his nonprofit must budget 10% to cover various sorts of corruption, mostly bribes and such. When that percentage rises steeply, not only can they not afford the money, but they cannot afford to complain — this is the point at which open objection can become dangerous. So his nonprofit has been working to use Tor to safely whistleblower on government corruption in order to continue their work.

At a recent conference, a Tor staffer ran into a woman who came from a "company town" in the eastern United States. She was attempting to blog anonymously to rally local residents to urge reform in the company that dominated the towns economic and government affairs. She is fully cognizant that the kind of organizing she was doing could lead to harm or "fatal accidents."

In east Asia, some labor organizers use anonymity to reveal information regarding sweatshops that produce goods for western countries and to organize local labor.

Tor can help activists avoid government or corporate censorship that hinders organization. In one such case, a

Canadian ISP blocked access to a union website used by their own employees to help organize a strike.

Why High & low profile people use Tor

Does being in the public spotlight shut you off from having a private life, forever, online? A rural lawyer in a New England state keeps an anonymous blog because, with the diverse clientele at his prestigious law firm, his political beliefs are bound to offend someone. Yet, he doesn't want to remain silent on issues he cares about. Tor helps him feel secure that he can express his opinion without consequences to his public role.

People living in poverty often don't participate fully in civil society -- not out of ignorance or apathy, but out of fear. If something you write were to get back to your boss, would you lose your job? If your social worker read about your opinion of the system, would she treat you differently? Anonymity gives a voice to the voiceless. Although it's often said that the poor do not use online access for civic engagement, failing to act in their self-interests, it is our hypothesis (based on personal conversations and anecdotal information) that it is precisely the "permanent record " left online that keeps many of the poor from speaking out on the Internet. We hope to show people how to engage more safely online, and then at the end of the year, evaluate how online and offline civic engagement has changed, and how the population sees this continuing into the future.

Why Business executives use Tor

Security breach information clearinghouses: Say a financial institution participates in a security clearinghouse of information on Internet attacks. Such a repository requires members to report breaches to a central group, who correlates attacks to detect coordinated patterns and send out alerts. But if a specific bank in St. Louis is breached, they don't want an attacker watching the incoming traffic to such a repository to be able to track where information is coming from. Even though every packet were encrypted, the IP address would betray the location of a compromised system.

Tor allows such repositories of sensitive information to resist compromises.

Seeing your competition as your market does: If you try to check out a competitor's pricing, you may find no information or misleading information on their web site. This is because their web server may be keyed to detect connections from competitors, and block or spread disinformation to your staff. Tor allows a business to view their sector as the general public would view it.

Keeping strategies confidential: An investment bank, for example, might not want industry snoopers to be able to track what web sites their analysts are watching. The strategic importance of traffic patterns, and the vulnerability of the surveillance of such data, is starting to be more widely recognized in several areas of the business world.

Accountability: In an age when irresponsible and unreported corporate activity has undermined multi-billion dollar businesses, an executive exercising true stewardship wants the whole staff to feel free to disclose internal malfeasance. Tor facilitates internal accountability before it turns into whistle blowing.

Bloggers use Tor

Frequently we hear about bloggers who are <u>sued</u> or <u>fired</u> for saying perfectly legal things online, in their blog.

We recommend the <u>EFF Legal Guide for Bloggers</u>.

Global Voices maintains a <u>guide to anonymous blogging with Wordpress and Tor</u>.

Why IT Professionals use Tor

To verify IP based firewall rules: A firewall may have some policies that only allow certain IP addresses or ranges. Tor can be used to verify those configurations by using an IP number outside of the company's allowed IP block.

To bypass their own security systems for sensitive professional activities: For instance, a company may have a strict policy regarding the material employees can view on the internet. A log review reveals a possible violation. Tor can be used to verify the information without an exception being put into corporate security systems.

To connect back to deployed services: A network engineer can use Tor to remotely connect back to services, without the need for an external machine and user account, as part of operational testing.

To access internet resources: Acceptable use policy for IT Staff and normal employees is usually different. Tor can allow unfettered access to the internet while leaving standard security policies in place.

To work around ISP network outages: Sometimes when an ISP is having routing or DNS problems, Tor can make internet resources available, when the actual ISP is malfunctioning. This can be invaluable tool in a crisis situations.

Like any technology, from pencils to cellphones, anonymity can be used for both good and bad. You have probably seen some of the vigorous debate (pro, con, and academic) over anonymity. The Tor project is based on the belief that anonymity is not just a good idea some of the time — it is a requirement for a free and functioning society. The EFF maintains a good overview of how anonymity was crucial to the founding of the United States. Anonymity is recognized by US courts as a fundamental and important right. In fact, governments mandate anonymity in many cases themselves: police tip lines, adoption services, police officer identities, and so forth. It would be impossible to rehash the entire anonymity debate here — it is too large an issue with too many nuances, and there are plenty of other places where this information can be found. We do have a Tor abuse page describing some of the possible abuse cases for Tor, but suffice it to say that if you want to abuse the system, you'll either find it mostly closed for your purposes (e.g. the majority of Tor relays do not support SMTP in order to prevent anonymous email spamming), or if you're one of the Four Horsemen of the Information Apocalypse, you have better options than Tor. While not dismissing the potential abuses of Tor, this page shows a few of the many important ways anonymity is used online today.

The Deep Dark Web – the hidden web

A Recon into the Abyss

What is the Deep Web? A first trip into the abyss

The Deep Web (or Invisible web) is the set of information resources on the World Wide Web not reported by normal **search engines**. According several researches the principal search engines index only a small portion of the overall web content, the remaining part is unknown to the majority of web users.

What do you think if you were told that under our feet, there is a world larger than ours and much more crowded? We will literally be shocked, and this is the reaction of those individual who can understand the existence of the Deep Web, a network of interconnected systems, are not indexed, having a size hundreds of times higher than the current web,

around 500 times.

Very exhaustive is the

Figure 18 - Representation of DeepWeb

BrightPlanet, Mike Bergman, that compared searching on the Internet today to dragging a net across the surface of the ocean: a great deal may be caught in the net, but there is a wealth of information that is deep and therefore missed.

Ordinary search engines to find content on the web using software called "crawlers". This technique is ineffective for finding the hidden resources of the Web that could be classified into the following categories:

1. ***Dynamic content***: dynamic pages which are returned in response to a submitted query or accessed only through a form, especially if open-domain input elements (such as text fields) are used; such fields are hard to navigate without domain knowledge.
2. ***Unlinked content***: pages, which are not linked to by other pages, which may prevent Web crawling programs from accessing the content. This content is referred to as pages without backlinks (or inlinks).
3. ***Private Web***: sites that require registration and login (password-protected resources).
   i. Contextual Web: pages with content varying for different access contexts (e.g., ranges of client IP addresses or previous navigation sequence).
4. ***Limited access content***: sites that limit access to their pages in a technical way (e.g., using the Robots Exclusion Standard, CAPTCHAs, or no-cache Pragma HTTP headers which prohibit search engines from browsing them and creating cached copies).
5. ***Scripted content***: pages that are only accessible through links produced by JavaScript as well as content dynamically downloaded from Web servers via Flash or Ajax solutions.
6. ***Non-HTML/text content***: textual content encoded in multimedia (image or video) files or specific file formats not handled by search engines.
7. ***Text content using the Gopher protocol and files hosted on FTP that are not indexed by most search engines***. Engines such as Google do not index pages outside of HTTP or HTTPS.

A parallel web that has a much wider number of information represents an invaluable resource for private companies, governments, and especially **cybercrime**. In the imagination of many persons, the Deep Web term is associated with the concept of anonymity that goes with criminal intents that cannot be pursued because submerged in an inaccessible world.

As we will see this interpretation of the Deep Web is deeply wrong, we are facing with a network definitely different from the usual web but in many ways repeats the same issues in a different sense.

What is a Tor? How to preserve the anonymity?

Tor is the acronym of "The onion router", a system implemented to enable online anonymity. Tor client software routes Internet traffic through a worldwide volunteer network of servers hiding user's information eluding any activities of monitoring.

As usually happen, the project was born in military sector, sponsored the US Naval Research Laboratory and from 2004 to 2005 it was supported by the Electronic Frontier Foundation.

Actually the software is under development and maintenance of Tor Project. A user that navigate using Tor it's difficult to trace ensuring his privacy because the data are encrypted multiple times passing through nodes, Tor relays, of the network.

Connecting to the Tor network

Imagine a typical scenario where Alice desire to be connected with Bob using the Tor network. Let's see step by step how it is possible.

She makes an **<u>unencrypted</u>** connection to a centralized directory server containing the addresses of Tor nodes. After receiving the address list from the directory server the Tor client software will connect to a random node (***the entry node***), through an encrypted connection. The entry node would make an **<u>encrypted</u>** connection to a random second node which would in turn do the same to connect to a random third Tor node. The process goes on until it involves a node (*exit node*) connected to the destination.

Consider that during Tor routing, in each connection, the Tor node are randomly chosen and the same node cannot be used twice in the same path.

To ensure anonymity the connections have a fixed duration. Every ten minutes to avoid statistical analysis that could compromise the user's privacy, the client software changes the entry node

Up to now we have considered an ideal situation in which a user accesses the network only to connect to another. To further complicate the discussion, in a real scenario, the node Alice could in turn be used as a node for routing purposes with other established connections between other users.

A malevolent third party would not be able to know which connection is initiated as a user and which as node making impossible the monitoring of the communications.

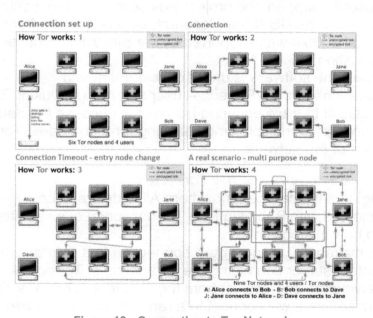

Figure 19 - Connection to Tor Network

After this necessary parenthesis on Tor network routing we are ready to enter the Deep Web simply using the Tor software from the official web site of the project. Tor is able to work on all the existing platforms and many add-ons make simple they integration in existing applications, including web browsers. Despite the network has been projected to protect user's privacy, to be really anonymous it's suggested to go through a VPN.

A better mode to navigate inside the deep web is to use the **Tails OS distribution** which is bootable from any machine don't leaving a trace on the host. Once the Tor Bundle is installed it comes with its own portable Firefox version, ideal for anonymous navigation due an appropriate control of installed plug-in, in the commercial version in fact common plug-in could expose our identity.

Once inside the network, where it possible to go and what is it possible to find?

Well once inside the deep web we must understand that the navigation is quite different from ordinary web, every research is more complex due the absence of indexing of the content.

A user that start it's navigation in the Deep Web have to know that a common way to list the content is to adopt collection of Wikis and BBS-like sites which have the main purpose to aggregate links categorizing them in more suitable groups of consulting. Another difference that user has to take in mind is that instead of classic extensions (e.g. .com, .gov) the domains in the Deep Web generally end with the .onion suffix.

Following a short list of links that have made famous the Deep Web published on **Pastebin**

The Deep Dark Web – the hidden web

Figure 20 - List of links in the Deep Web

Cleaned Hidden Wiki should be a also a good starting point for the first navigations

http://3suaolltfj2xjksb.onion/hiddenwiki/index.php/Main_Page
Be careful, some content are labeled with common used tag such as CP= child porn, PD is pedophile, stay far from them.

The Deep Web is considered the place where everything is possible, you can find every kind of material and services for sale, most of them illegal. The hidden web offers to cybercrime great business opportunity, hacking **services**, malware, stolen credit cards, weapons.

We all know the potentiality of the e-commerce in ordinary web and its impressive growth in last couple of years, well now imagine the Deep Web market that is more than 500 times bigger and where there is no legal limits on the odds to sell. We are facing with amazing business controlled by cybercriminal organizations.

Speaking of dark market we cannot avoid to mention Silk Road web site, an online marketplace located in the Deep Web, the majority of its products are derived from illegal activities. Of course it's not the only one, many other markets are managed to address specify products, believe me, many of them are terrifying.

Most transactions on the Deep Web accept **BitCoin** system

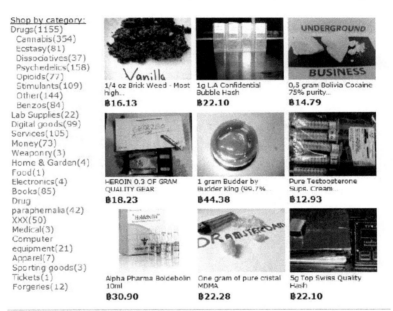

for payments allowing the purchase of any kind of products preserving the anonymity of the transaction, encouraging the development of t

Figure 21 - Silk Road web site

of illegal activitie.. ... ...

system that advantage the exercise of criminal activities while ensuring the anonymity of transactions and the inability to track down the criminals.

But is it really all-anonymous? Is it possible to be traced in the Deep Web? What is the position of the governments towards the Deep Web?

Hacktivist and Dissidents Online

The hacktivism phenomenon

In today's society technology plays a crucial role and is used as a new cultural vehicle, and even aggregation element or carrier to express dissent against the policies of governments and private companies.

Groups such as Anonymous are maximum expression of a phenomenon defined "Hacktivism" that refers the usage of computers and computer networks to express social protest or to promote political ideology. This form of protest is not new, the term in fact was introduced for the first time in 1996 by a member of famous group of hackers the Cult of the Dead Cow hacker named Omega. The Hacktivist use to attack systems and architectures with legal and illegal tools to manifest their dissent through cyber attacks such as denial-of-service attacks, information theft, data breach, web site defacement, Typo-Squatting and any other methods of digital sabotage. Forms of hacktivism are carried out in the belief that proper use of the technical tools will be able to produce similar results to those produced by regular activism

The Virtual Wars: How **HACKTIVISM** Finally Became a Powerful Virtual Weapon

Hacktivism is defined as "the nonviolent use of legal and/or illegal digital tools in pursuit of political ends"

or civil disobedience to promote political ideology.

Anonymous collective is now the incarnation of the hacktivism concept that has monopolized the worldwide attention on the phenomenon.
We must consider that Internet world is profoundly changing due the continuous acts of hacktivism, the related operations represents one of the major cyber threats today. The attacks of these groups produced the same effects of those perpetrated by cyber criminals or governments to offend strategic objectives, for these reasons cyber protest must be taken into serious consideration in cyber strategies for the defense of a nation.
According the study "Data Breach Investigations Report"

Figure 22 - Hacktivism manifest

(http://www.verizonbusiness.com/resources/reports/rp_data-breach-investigations-report-2012_en_xg.pdf), published by Verizon, Hacktivist stole almost twice as many records of ordinary cybercrime from organizations and government agencies.

Table 5. Varieties of external agents by percent of breaches within External and percent of records

	All Orgs		Larger Orgs	
Organized criminal group	83%	35%--	33%	36%
Unknown	10%	1%	31%	0%
Unaffiliated person(s)	4%	0%	10%	0%
Activist group	2%	58%+	21%	61%
Former employee (no longer had access)	1%	0%	6%	0%
Relative or acquaintance of employee	0%	0%	2%	0%

Figure 23 - Data published on Verizon Report

WHO IS BEHIND DATA BREACHES?	HOW DO BREACHES OCCUR?
98% stemmed from external agents (+6%)	**81%** utilized some form of hacking (+31%)
4% implicated internal employees (-13%)	**69%** incorporated malware (+20%)
	10% involved physical attacks (-19%)
<1% committed by business partners (◊)	**7%** employed social tactics (-4%)
58% of all data theft tied to activist groups	**5%** resulted from privilege misuse (-12%)

Figure 24 - Data published on Verizon Report on Data Breaches

The most significant change we saw in 2011 was the rise of "hacktivism" against larger organizations worldwide. An impressive number of attacks made by activists with regular frequency have been registered during last year causing a great deal of effort responding to the cyber threat. The type attacks more diffused is without doubts the Distributed Denial of Service (DDoS) attack, which attempt to make a site or service unavailable to its users due an enormous quantity of request sent in a short period. Hacktivist are demonstrating increasing skills in their attacks and we expect increasing in number of their operations with possible extensive damage.

In the past, Anonymous supporters have used a program called LOIC allowing them to join in an attack on a particular website, flooding it with unwanted traffic, the group has also released on the web instructions and videos on how to conduct this king of operations. In terms of media Anonymous group can be a lesson to many. However, the latest attack I believe represents an element of further development for the group, although it is always a DDoS type, the method used has profoundly changed in the conception.

The recruitment campaign for the attack has also served major social media being able to engage in this way an impressive number of participants with devastating consequences for victims. Hence the web and social networks like Facebook and Twitter have been flooded by messages of affiliates to the group. Anonymous in this way has raised the bar, even a user without his knowledge by simply visiting a web page without him interaction, has started to flood a victim with unwanted traffic. The trick is possible simply hiding within the web pages procedures JavaScript developed specifically that the web browser interprets, the unique defense option is to disable JavaScript in the browser.

Hacktivism has made a quantum leap with this new method for two simple reasons:

- The first is that without a doubt the offensive force has increased dramatically.
- The second, more subtle but formidable in my opinion, is that from a legal standpoint it is hardly attributable to each user a criminal liability. A user who participates in the attack, unlike what happened before with Loic, today could not always claim to be aware. This subtle aspect could be stimulus for a wide category of undecided who share the ideology of the fear of incurring legal process by participating in operations.

The cyber war between governments and groups of Hacktivist such as Anonymous has an important social connotation, popular movements that through technology show their disagreement and fight for the conquest of freedom. The fight for freedom of expression, the total aversion to any form of control and monitoring, reporting of abuse of power and blatant violations are the main arguments that incite to the action groups of Hacktivist, however, the boundary between interpretation of an operation as a simple act of protest or as cybercrime is thin. While many operations are limited to DDoS against few web sites in more than one occasion, the disclosure of information acquired through hacking systems have exposed sensitive data to public opinions with serious consequences.

It's happened last Christmas when Wikileaks has published with the support of Anonymous more than five millions of email from Texas-based global security think tank company Stratfor, a global intelligence firm.
WikiLeaks and Anonymous, a strategic partnership between the major expressions of hacktivism culture, two forces that together are able to frighten the world's great, the new alliance against dirty affairs. The hack of the Stratfor Global Intelligence service was made by the same collective Anonymous who disclosed company website and also the full client list of over 4000 individuals and corporations. They gained access to a subscriber list stored on stratfor.com, and that list contained unencrypted credit card data of the customers. The published email demonstrate that Stratfor company was providing confidential intelligence services to several corporations, such as Lockheed Martin, and also to government agencies such as the US Department of Homeland Security, the US Marines and the US Defense Intelligence Agency. The exposed material shows how Government and diplomatic sources all around the world give Stratfor firm advance knowledge of the events and of the politic strategies, all in exchange for money. A great spider of informants, government employees, embassy staff and journalists, recruited in everywhere and paid through Swiss banks accounts and pre-paid credit cards. The mutual cooperation had already been manifested when the Anonymous group opposed to the actions tied against the founder of Wikileaks Assange accused of publishing hundreds of Thousands of secret U.S. government cables beginning in December 2010. The US government applied as penalty the block of economic support to the group and PayPal, MasterCard and Visa blocked payments to WikiLeaks, which relied on donations to lease infrastructures. To protest against the penalty, Anonymous arranged massive attacks against these financial institutions. Of course the actions of groups of Hacktivist represent a serious threat to private industry and the national security of each country. The group's attacks have been shown to bring the blocking of services provided by a company, to gain

access to sensitive information whose disclosure could undermine the internal balance of a country and its relationship with allied states. And it's for this reason that hacktivism is considered within a cyber strategy a major cyber threats that can cripple with his attacks critical infrastructures, financial services and government agencies. Groups of Hacktivist are considered as uncontrollable variables in the cyber space capable of surprising us with striking operations worthy of the most skilled cyber army.

Who really takes advantage of the operations of Anonymous?

The last few years to consolidate its image Anonymous has become one of the most debated phenomenon on internet, many consider the collective Anonymous a threat, many other the expression of a dissent to listen. Both interpretations are correct, but let's think for a moment to the misuse of the name Anonymous, who and why can bring in the fame of the famous group of hackers?

Are we really able to fight against the hacktivism and do we desire do it?

It's true that the raise of hacktivism in the last 4 years has created several problems to governments and private firms, but it also true that many figures have benefited of the operation promoted by Anonymous.

First of all many security firms have had the opportunity to promote their services and solutions to protect companies from the attacks of collective, for example DDoS attacks have become famous after the first attacks made by Anonymous, with their popularity is increased the sold for network appliances able to secure prevent the destruction of web services or data breach.

Again we can consider the intelligence services provided to prevent the clamorous operation of the hackers and to expose the identities of members of the collective, several

Figure 25 - Anonymous manifest

private agencies have sold their reports and advices to law enforcement and private businesses, we speak of flourishing business!

But in many cases the reality exceed fiction, the governments seems to be the entities that can most benefit of the hacktivism. Last year I wrote on the possible usage of Anonymous as cyber weapon trying to explain how foreign

government could conduct covert operations, such as cyber attacks or cyber espionage in the name of the group or influencing the choices of the Anonymous.

Several operations of Anonymous have attacked networks and web site belonging to governments, it's happened for example with #OpChina and #opJapan, when the hackers have targeted the two countries to officially protest against censorship and web monitoring.

This offensive scenarios could advantage a state sponsored attacks, attackers could benefit of the rumors of the attacks to bypass security protection stressed by the events. In this case group of hackers could follow the organization of an event that represents for them a diversion option, a lapse time in which the adversary protection are engaged against attacks coming from other sources.

Well this in my opinion the most plausible scenario, but not the only one.

In other situation governments could be in interested to put the blame on Anonymous while they remain hidden, we are living in the era of cyber war and the operations in cyberspace are joining more and more frequently conventional military operations.

For example some experts believe that the #opChina could be also be supported by foreign governments like US or other western countries, Rob Rachwald, directory of security strategy at Imperva, doesn't exclude the participation of governments in the attack declaring:

"It was a pretty extensive campaign. Could it be the US government helping out? I don't know, [but] I wouldn't rule it out. Could it be German, UK hackers sponsored by the government? I don't know."

Many skeptics may argue then why the collective Anonymous in this case leaves governments to act with impunity. Possible explanations could be the intent to don't be catch in a potential trap set for to come forward them, we have also hypothesize that the same Anonymous benefits in terms of media exposure in a time where its operations have triggered a process of habituation, but the most plausible thesis is in the inability of a central collective to validate and monitor attacks made by various groups all over the world.

The common trend to underestimate Anonymous groups may conceal other intentions, the desire of governments to be able to infiltrate the Hacktivist influencing their policies and strategies. The governments know well the potential of their cyber threats, despite they represent a serious danger, they prefer to avoid a direct confrontation, there are no serious offensives of intelligence against the collective operations that have not been a response to an attack. Yes we often read of sporadic arrests that actually represent a sop to the collectivity, Anonymous must continue to operate, there are too much conveniences to stop them.

Nobody really know identities of these individuals that fight for freedom and internet rights, but what is indisputable is their offensive power. I'm not speaking of DDoS attacks but the effected related to various data breach they conducted. China taught the world the importance of cyber espionage, discovery the enemy secrets, to steal their intellectual property, well all this attacks could benefit of the Anonymous brand. Governments can masquerade their identities hacking foreign networks, they could infiltrate groups of Hacktivist acquiring sensible information, in many cases in fact following data breach the disclosed data have been used for further attacks such as APT and other targeted offensive.
In light of all the above reflection are we really sure that there is imminent need to eradicate Anonymous?

The social dissent in the Deep Web

When we think of hacktivism phenomenon immediately we connect it to the anonymity, in fact, those who for various reasons wish to express their dissent more often prefer the use of anonymity. It's clear that the ultimate context in which these people can freely exchange ideas and information is the DeepWeb.

We have got to in the preceding paragraphs to understand the structure of the Deep Web and the way in which services are provided allowing the user through simple steps, to preserve their right to anonymity.

It's true that hacktivism is a movement based on the involvement of critical masses of individuals that share the reason of the protest but many experts believe that groups such as Anonymous are led by a restricted pool of specialists who have a deep knowledge of computers science, maybe most of them are also members of primary corporate or governmental agencies. These specialists are one of the most active current of the Dark Web, many consider these professionals as the equivalent of today's Carbonari motions. Hacktivist are interested to Deep Web not only because they need secure communication platform but also because they are also active in this cyber space. We must distinguish two different participative approaches to the Dark Web, hacktivism in fact could surf in the hidden space for information gathering purpose, the "passive mode", and also in active mode conducing cyber operation similar to ones promoted in the ordinary web. The #OPDarknet has revealed in the end of 2011 over 1500 accounts from trading website for pedophiles hosted in the deep web. In that occasion Anonymous published as usually a communicate on Pastebin explains that their campaign manifested upon finding a Hidden Wiki listing called "Hard Candy" that they say "was dedicated to links to child pornography."

During the operation where noted that most of the pedophile-content sites listed on the Hidden Wiki, "shared a digital

fingerprint with the shared hosting server at Freedom Hosting", due to this reason Anonymous declared war to the hosting service that ignores denunciation of the collective. October 14th 2011, Anonymous invited Freedom Hosting to remove all the pedo links from its server, but they ignored this so the group of hackers responded by attacking and taking down the server in more than one occasion.
The fight against child pornography continued with further attacks against other another Hidden Wiki listing, a file-swapping site used by pedophiles called "Lolita City".

Footsteps of the Hacktivist

<u>Sample of Communication Channels</u>
The deep web is an ocean of information, and to find the right way in this world is to a first approach may seem very complicated, but with good will and some evidence from the earliest voyages is possible to obtain satisfactory results.
Of course the communication platforms such as social networks are, as in the classic web as, the deep web privileged places where groups can exchange messages Hacktivist, for example a micro blogger twitter like for the

onion world that is frequented by many Hacktivist is
TorStatusNet - lotjbov3gzzf23hc.onion
(http://lotjbov3gzzf23hc.onion/index.php/).

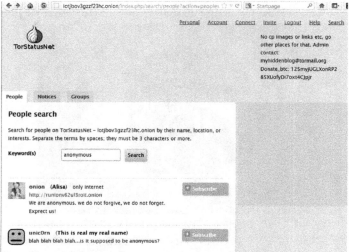

Figure 27 - TorStatusNet - lotjbov3gzzf23hc.onion

It only remains to eavesdrop and intercept any message that
could lead to some hidden service set up by supporters of
the organization.
Another interesting communication platform is the USA
based FREEFOR (http://tns7i5gucaaussz4.onion/) that
implements a turnkey distributed Temporary Autonomous
Zone to provide secure and anonymous communication to
Liberty oriented individuals. Similar platforms are often used
by groups of Hacktivist that continuously change
communication channel to avoid any kind of tracking and
interception.
The platform provides Forum and Wiki services, and of
course a chat for free communication after registration.
Continuing the theme is common to find groups of Hacktivist
that communicate also posting on social networks within the
Deep Web, an example is provided by the platform
Mul.Tiver.se (http://ofrmtr2fphxkqgz3.onion/)

The Deep Dark Web – the hidden web

Figure 28 - Mul.Tiver.se Social Network

Another place in the deep web where to find interesting interventions on the themes debated by hacktivism movements is TorDir The link list /AND PM SYSTEM/ of Tor (http://dppmfxaacucguzpc.onion/index.php?sid=jp3ov0726n1sqh5 nm53iqi8ni7).

The site is well organized proposing several categories of content such as Activism, Political and Revolutionary. It contains also many links related to communication platforms and contents posted by several exponent of the phenomenon.

Figure 29 - TorDir

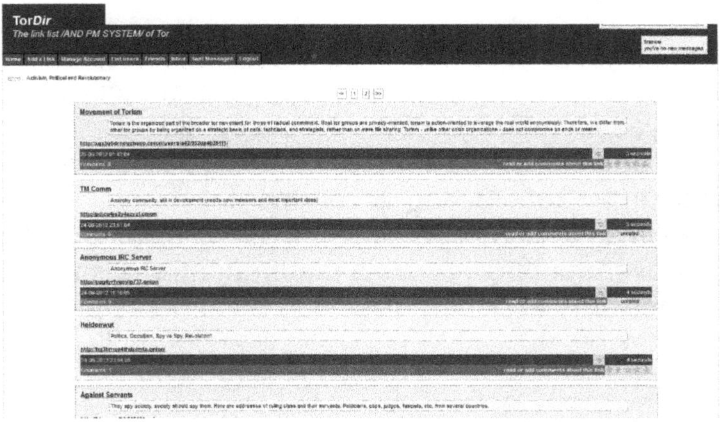

These sites are font of inspiration for several groups of activist that thanks to these services could have an anonymity access to precious resources on intelligence and politics.

Among social dissent and complaint

The concept of hacktivism bride that promotes the social criticism, however, is not simply expose information that may be compromising safety and that surely can endanger those who wish to disclose.

We all know Wikileaks and its founder Julian Assange, the not-for-profit organization publishing submissions of private,

secret, and classified media from anonymous news sources, news leaks, and whistleblowers. Assange is an activist by definition, was found guilty of disclosing confidential documents and compromising its policy regarding the conduct of organizations and governments.

Deep Web is a precious source to collect compliant on illicit made by governments, there is a huge quantity of sites that give the possibility to publish reserved documents preserving the anonymity of
the submitter.

Deep web is recognized as a powerful instrument to share and divulgate compromising files, it represents an option to everybody that desire to disclose document being anonymous.

The practice of hacktivism also contemplates the use of dark web for sharing information and consultation of the sources in total anonymity.

During the last week Vatican faces a widening scandal that has seen Pope Benedict's butler arrested, the president of its bank unceremoniously dismissed and the publication of a new book alleging conspiracies among cardinals ... but what is happened in the darkweb? Without going in the deep I propose the graph of the connected Vatican users that demonstrates the relationship with the events.

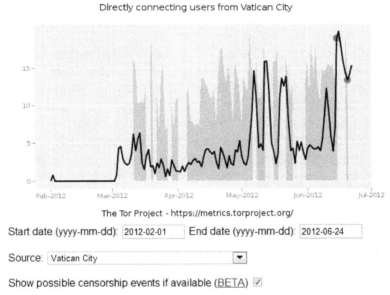

Figure 31 - Connected user during Vatican leaks

Deep Web as inspiration source

When we speak of hacktivism in reality, we exemplify the very concept of social dissent as it is known that can be expressed in various forms and can be addressed to specific social issues. We talked for instance of child pornography, politics, intelligence, but the phenomenon is extremely

complex and subject of the disagreement may also be religious institutions or nonprofit organizations.
Wander around the web in search of dark politics, occultism, Spy vs. Spy and Revolution topics we can meet the site "Heidenwut" (http://hq3hmoa4thdplmta.onion/) whose disclaimer reads:

"This site is for those interested in effective revolutionary strategies, occultism, politics, and all other things in regards to overthrowing the system that we have all come to hate. I, Heiden the webmaster of this site am one of the few people on Tor who really need to be on the Undernet. Which means that this site is not just another right or left wing whine-fest nor the millionth re-post of the anarchist cookbook."

The web site proposes a lot of stuff not only related to hacktivism, but it is considered a precious source of information for those all minds that search for uncomfortable truths that could inspire their operations.
It's well known that one of the fundamental of hacktivism is the free circulation of ideas, freedom of expression and the inalienable right to anonymity, so let me suggest, to who want to know more about the hacktivism thought, to site visit BuggedPlanet.Info, where is possible to retrieve interesting info on Telecommunication Interception Companies & Installations (http://6sgjmi53igmg7fm7.onion/).
The site is a precious source of information categorized and proposed for geographical location, it also collects a serious of useful articles, event information and situations that give to the reader a clear situation of the real status of control and surveillance in each country.
In the dark web every Hacktivist is able to share contents, to participate to open dialogue on specific themes and could be informed on the operation proposed by various collective.
The Deep web is full of material on the most different topics, the anonymity represents a powerful flywheel for the free circulation of the information exist but also the reverse of the medal, it is quite simple in fact find web site characterized by very questionable content.

A Hacktivist could use the hidden web as source for his researches but it can also be interested to investigate in cybercrimes that insults human dignity such as pedophilia. It's difficult to believe that this content can be of inspiration for movements that express their dissent through the usage of technology, in the deep web the control is weak and anyone can disseminate information designed to manipulate events and situations. The real risk is the loss of meaning of the information due its inflation, the risk is very high.
The world is in constant and tumultuous protest, simply choose your battle and grapple with the proposed options.

   Not only Anonymous
Members of the famous collective haven't a specific place where to share the information, platforms such as TorStatusNet represent a good system to communicate like they usually do in the clear web using twitter. Simple and short messages exchanged to refer public or covert information.
Interesting the group of discussion lulzfinancial http://lotjbov3gzzf23hc.onion/index.php/tag/lulzfinancial used by Anonymous followers to exchange ideas and information. Another interesting place where Anonymous store information regarding people involved in the situation the use to debate is DOXBIN (http://npieqpvpjhrmdchg.onion/doxviewer.php#). The site proposes a huge quantity of information regarding very interesting people, including private information such as composition of their families. The documents have personal cards format where the Hacktivist define the targets and their alleged offenses.
The Deep Web is also considered by the group of Hacktivist the right place where to publish the data leaked during their operation, let's me remind you for example the case of the "HBGary Federal Attachment Dump" , the email archive leaked by Anonymous is consultable at the following address http://xqz3u5drneuzhaeo.onion/users/hbgary/ . It's strongly recommended to do not download files from the hidden web

without proper precautions, so download the file on a virtual environment and test it.

Despite Anonymous is considered the icon of the hacktivism many other groups use the Deep Web to arrange their political operations and promoting new ideas and form of protest, one of them is the Movement of Torism (http://xqz3u5drneuzhaeo.onion/users/a42/932da4b351f1/), an organized group of the broader tor movement that defines itself "action-oriented" to defend the right to the anonymity. Torism is working with other action groups, but its organization appear similar to other group of activist, but they declare to have a peer structure, without leaders: "There are no leaders. Freedom in action follows from freedom in theory"

The group declared also to have a medium range goal of defense of the counter-economy, also called the underground free market, to fight for a society of free trade in goods and values.

Some specialists believe that Movement of Torism is the interface between existing anonymous organizations and the real world, it is one of the main groups that promote the concept of anarchy, against the State centric vision.

The topics proposed are aimed to illustrate the potential of Deep Web for Hacktivist groups, explaining how they can use services and resources to share valuable information and to communicate in anonymity.

The relationship between hacktivism and anonymity is extremely strong for obvious reason, a careful analysis of the Hidden Web could lead a more experienced reader to the startling revelations on uncomfortable truths... enjoy the trip.

How to mitigate the risks of exposure to hacktivism attacks?

The cornerstone of the hacktivism is the recruitment of common people through social media to engage in protests, no matter if it happen in ordinary web or in the deep web, it's powerful machine that moves announcing its arrival and producing a loud noise. This undoubtedly provides a serious of advantages to the targets and to law enforcement.

The proclamations of the groups give indications on the attacks, such as targets and timing information, thanks to this data governments and law enforcement agencies can map the offensive of the group qualifying the cyber threat and its impact. Governments have accelerated the implementation of measures to control the main channels of communication adopted by Hacktivist in the clear web, but many operations are also conducted in the hidden web tracking participations and discussions on the principal services used by the hackers. Monitoring systems of increasingly powerful have been implemented and are being acquired to correlate events and activities within main social media and search engines, the scope is to collect huge quantity of info on the past attacks and correlating them with incoming events trying to limit the exposure to the attacks.

Is hacktivism only a threat or also a voice to listen?
Some forms of protest are for sure illegal but we must consider that they are expression of dissent shared between large communities, they are the voice of masses. The demonstration is inside the number behind each attack, these guys are not alone, and they have a lot of common people behind. The main events of protest in the history were always characterized by elements of illegality due their connotation of opposing the governments in question. From legislative perspective we must distinguish Hacktivist from cyber criminals.
Anonymous is the social structure, daughter of the technology, with the ability to intervene on the digital infrastructure that support the digital world today. It is an instrument of power of the people and must to be considered as such.
The minds behind Anonymous have the potential to jeopardize the stability of the world, today the government websites have been compromised and what would happen if the next time they were being targeted critical infrastructure?

We must consider the reasons on genesis of this type of movements, otherwise we will not have framed what I consider a historical phenomenon.

In terms of security, the group is without doubt to be considered as a threat due the capabilities shown and objectives selected, politically I think that Anonymous is a voice to be taken into account. Ideologies do not repress it with the arrests.

What to expect from the future?

These attacks observed should lead us to some reflections, I think the group is a time of transition, despite having reached a critical mass of supporters began to split into numerous cells scattered throughout the world. For now, these cells appear to be driven by common goals, but what will happen tomorrow? In a heterogeneous scenario the risk that external agents can infiltrate the group influencing policy is concrete.

New operations can be organized in the name of the group with unpredictable consequences, foreign states or law enforcement may involve masses of people and convinced unaware Hacktivist to conduct ideological battles.

What guarantees the group can provide to its supporters? Will the core of the group like Anonymous be able to capillary check any communication made globally with its brand? Of course not!

I think for this reason that the groups of Hacktivist should change their strategies, they are obliged to appear in new forms, probably in the future presented itself to the world with their representatives. The time of hiding, in the form of protest could begin to decline. The groups are aware that their attacks may begin to serve to a third cause, not only their own. Analyzing for example the Anonymous case, we must distinguish two phases of Anonymous phenomenon, the first one that I define "*Here I am, know me and learn to live with my judgment*" is the one we are leaving, in this phase the group introduced himself to the world, showing their offensive capabilities but also a broad support enjoyed by. The second phase, named "*Openness*", is the one we will live in the next months, in this phase the group will tries to try to talk with institutions, will operate on internet but also in the street. The stage is very delicate because of the heterogeneous nature of the groups, many Hacktivist will not accept the openness to institutions becoming active in a loose, loose cannons in the web that could stage striking and unethical attacks.

This is the worst scenario, the web may soon reign in the chaos and regulations such as the one under discussion certainly would not be able to govern.

Anonymous, Wikileaks and evolution of hacktivism

In the last months we have assisted of an intensification of the operations that we common locate under the hacktivism umbrella. Millions of people claim freedom of internet access and the respect of human rights. The right to Internet access, also known as the right to broadband, states that all individuals must be able to access the Internet in order to exercise and enjoy their rights to Freedom of expression and opinion and other fundamental human rights. In many countries such as France, Spain and Finland Internet access is already considered a final human right. Unfortunately that not true all over the world, in industrialized as in totalitarian regimes, with the unique differences that in the second categories the control and surveillance of internet causes the persecution of millions of dissidents every year. The world is rapidly changing thanks to technologies, and new media such as internet represents privileged platforms to develop social debate on every kind of topic, limiting the access to the network today means limit freedom of expression of the citizens of the world. Let's me highlight some of the "Recommendations of the UN Special Reporter (2011)" that clarifies the role of internet in the today's society and establishes a duty for all states to ensure free access to the network of its own citizens. The report establishes the promotion and protection of the right to freedom of opinion and expression:

- *67. Unlike any other medium, the Internet enables individuals to seek, receive and impart information and ideas of all kinds instantaneously and inexpensively across national borders. By vastly expanding the capacity of individuals to enjoy their right to freedom of opinion and expression, which is an "enabler" of other human rights, the Internet boosts economic, social and political development, and contributes to the progress of humankind as a whole. In this regard, the Special Reporter encourages other Special Procedures mandate holders to engage on the issue of the Internet with respect to their particular mandates.*
- *78. While blocking and filtering measures deny users access to specific content on the Internet, States have also taken measures to cut off access to the Internet entirely. The Special Reporter considers cutting off users from Internet access, regardless of the justification provided, including on the grounds of violating intellectual property rights law, to be disproportionate and thus a violation of article 19, paragraph 3, of the International Covenant on Civil and Political Rights.*
- *79. The Special Reporter calls upon all States to ensure that Internet access is maintained at all times, including during times of political unrest.*
- *85. Given that the Internet has become an indispensable tool for realizing a range of human rights, combating inequality, and accelerating development and human progress, ensuring universal access to the Internet should be a priority for all States. Each State should thus develop a concrete and effective policy, in consultation with individuals from all sections of society, including the private sector and relevant Government ministries, to make the Internet widely available, accessible and affordable to all segments of population.*

Groups of Hacktivist are increasing the frequency of attacks against private companies and institutions guilty for choices and policies that are detrimental to the people of the net. The topics discussed are the most disparate, from opposition to regulations that attempt to regulate the network to shared bitter battle against pedophilia, all without neglecting social issues of current interest such as the defense of environment. Seeking to frame with the word "Anonymous" such a diverse ideologies is wrong, every day we are confronted with social issues often uncomfortable and in many cases in passively way. Controversial battles of the collective deserves credit for raising uncomfortable questions otherwise kept confined in the knowledge of a few, hacktivism is a source of serious concerns and considerable as a cyber threat but to these phenomena must also be recognized the social function of the debate. Often operations are egregious, questionable actions, but still represent the expression of a thought shared by huge masses.

Is it right to associate indissolubly the term hacktivism to cyber attacks and systems hacking?

We've had several attacks of Anonymous group recently, first against the Japanese government's policy and his willingness to stiffen penalties against the violation of copyright (#opjapan), then by association with Wikileaks was started disclosures of the famous Syria Files, unpleasant truths that bind to Western companies to bloodthirsty regimes. But as mentioned, under the name Anonymous are also recorded other operations against organizations of pedophiles (#OpPedoChat) and against companies responsible of environmental damage such as Russian oil firms Gazprom and Rosneft accused of melting the Arctic ice caps.

The preferred attack techniques adopted is the hack instead the classic DDoS attack with publication of email and other compromising documents, we must consider this approach that appears like the will of the collective to show to the world the dirty affairs instead to attack destroying something.

The difference is thin but meaningful, Anonymous seems to declare
"if you have nothing to hide, you haven't to fear Anonymous".
While the policy pursued by Anonymous maybe shareable we must consider the damage that such operations may cause:

- to the investigations of law enforcement who risk seeing hazy months or years of stalking.
- to ordinary people doing their work on behalf of multinationals are exposed to risks and retaliation. Take the case of Finmeccanica and Syria Files, some of the people involved in the exchanges of emails simply did the work that was asked them. Today some of these people have received threats by mail, and this is unfair and prejudicial, goes against the ideals of the group.

Hacktivism is a struggle for justice, fight the "reasons of state" who have planted more death and destruction of weapons, a little noticed work in my opinion could affect the future of movements that are fighting for freedom of expression and the right to Internet.

On the collaboration with WikiLeaks
Surely working with Wikileaks is a time of growth
for both organizations, I think we can expect a different "modus operandi" in the coming months, at least for the operations carried out by affiliates are very close to the Anonymous collective. The change lies in the mode of attack, probably I'm wrong, but the attacks have increasingly connotation of whistleblowers, events designed to stimulate greater public involvement than underperforming DDoS. The use of DDoS attacks may be limited situations where is meant to stop a service that is deemed harmful, such as diffusion of child porno material, or in situations when the hacking fails.

The influence of Wikileaks has produced its effect , Anonymous collective has launched in March its WikiLeaks like site called Par:AnoIA (Potentially Alarming Research: Anonymous Intelligence Agency). The site is promoted as a centralized storage for leaked documents to propose to the public.

*"The reason no one cares about these leaks, as a general rule of thumb, is that they can't **do** anything with [them],"* said a Paranoia anon volunteering on document processing for the project in an online chat with Wired. "Basically, [we're] making it accessible to anyone that wants to do something with it, in a proper usable format."

Of course as in every marriage there are threads, the promoting of a similar platform has for example annoyed Wikileaks exponents, mainly because they could be controlled by government and intelligence agencies, WikiLeaks in fact accused one of the main Anonymous Twitter accounts of advertising proxies running at the direction of law enforcement.

Figure 32 - Par:AnoIA (Potentially Alarming Research: Anonymous Intellig

An ambitious objective is the involvement of the masses

POTENTIALLY ALARMING RESEARCH

ANONYMOUS INTELLIGENCE AGENCY

Par:AnoIA

in the analysis of leaked data and not only in attacks

This aspect represents the real innovation, the collective desire to involve people in the collection and analysis of the sensible documents creating an open intelligence platform based on the contribution of common people, a sort of popular consciousness expressing his opinion openly and anonymously about news events.

Anonymous has already tried to setup a similar model of collaboration in the past promoting the #OperationLeakspin, but the experiment hasn't had success because the contributions came mainly from elements belonging to news agencies and security analysts. This time the collective desires major participation of common people counting on the great popularity of the group and better technological instruments for document sharing in anonymity.

Imagine the media coverage of this initiative, millions of people could process GBs of confidential documents stolen during an attack such as the hack of HB Gary Federal, thus multiplying the channels of dissemination of the news and making impossible the tracing of primary source, is just scary!

Everyone have to analyze the phenomenon of hacktivism in different perspectives and especially considering it as a model evolving. The error that security experts make most frequently is that they concern mainly the mechanism of cause / effect of each attack, completely ignoring the reasons behind it and the related media impact. The collateral damage of an attack can be more serious of the attack itself, the hype of an initiative could have a major effect of the result of a hack. The collective knows this, he first understood the need to involve the masses and show them the themes that are too often deliberately covered up. Movements such as Anonymous, grow, change and who is still wrong to expect the usual DDoS, the future of hacktivism is elsewhere. In many countries collective promoters of free movement of information are being organized in the form of a political party, the Hacktivist is not just a hacker is shifting closer to the masses under other garments.
We are in a period of great changes and groups as Anonymous also will evolve.

Legality of Anonymity

The right to anonymity on Internet and legal implications

Everyday all our web actions leave traces of ourselves and of our way of life through the storing of massive amounts of personal data in databases in the internet, all this information compose our **digital identity**, our representation in the cyber space.

Users are "entities" in the cyberspace, built also with the correlation of data that increasingly escapes the control of the owner, anyone can theoretically "expropriate" of our digital identity.

Not only that, in fact, certain personal information, even socially harmful, may be available to anyone beyond the time limits dictated by the principle of finality of the data, but also, even if such data were deleted, they may still be accessible through mechanisms storage such as "cached".

Today tracking user activities on internet are one of the primary **interests** for private companies and Governments, business and political motivations are pushing on the development of **monitoring** and surveillance systems. Let's consider that monitoring implemented by many **governments** in situation of political dissent have has serious consequences for dissidents that have been tracked and **persecuted** thanks to the **censorship**.

In response to rising of monitoring of the networks it has been observed the increasing of the demand of anonymity on the web, but the anonymity is a concept that induces fear in our mind because we tend to associate it to illicit activities and **cybercrimes**. This consideration is profoundly wrong, the anonymity of the user's participation on internet could be also motivated by right arguments, such as the fight for human right to liberty of expression, avoidance of censorship, liberal promotion and circulation of the thought.

The implementation of internet filters and anonymity are closely related, whereas the filters are applied at the network in a stringent and pervasive censorship, the possibility of being able to look out on an anonymous network becomes, first and foremost, a matter exercise of fundamental rights. Anonymous communications have an important place in our political and social discourse, many individuals desire to hide their identities because they may be concerned about political or economic retribution harassment or even threats to their lives.

Anonymity is derived from the Greek word *anonymia*, meaning "without a name", in the common usage the term refers to the state of an individual's personal identity, or personally identifiable information, being publicly unknown. In internet the anonymity is guaranteed when IP addresses cannot be tracked, due this reason it has been assisted to the creation of Anonymizing services such as **I2P** – The Anonymous Network or **Tor** address. The anonymizing services are based on the concept of distribution of routing information, during a transmission in fact is not known prior the path between source and destination and every node of the network manage minimal information to route the packets to the next hop without conserving history on the path, the introduction of encryption algorithms make impossible the wiretapping of the information and the recomposition of the original messages.

Right to anonymity – Legal implications

The Supreme Court of the United States has ruled repeatedly that the right to anonymous free speech is protected by the First Amendment. A much-cited 1995 Supreme Court ruling in McIntyre v. Ohio Elections Commission reads:

Protections for anonymous speech are vital to democratic discourse. Allowing dissenters to shield their identities frees them to express critical minority views . . . Anonymity is a shield from the tyranny of the majority. . . . It thus exemplifies the purpose behind the Bill of Rights and of the First

Amendment in particular: to protect unpopular individuals from retaliation . . . at the hand of an intolerant society.

Many institutions and foundations, such as **The Electronic Frontier Foundation**, are spending a great effort to protect the rights to on line anonymity. As one court observed in a case handled by EFF along with the ACLU of Washington:

"[T]he free exchange of ideas on the Internet is driven in large part by the ability of Internet users to communicate anonymously."

These organizations have challenged many efforts providing financial support to the development and deployment of Internet communications system to preserve anonymous communications, a valid example is the TOR network.

US First Amendment settled that the right to speak anonymously, the Supreme Court has held,

"Anonymity is a shield from the tyranny of the majority," that "exemplifies the purpose" of the First Amendment: "to protect unpopular individuals from retaliation…at the hand of an intolerant society."

Court pronunciations establish the duty for government to guard against undue hindrances to political conversations and the exchange of ideas, a vigilant review that "must be undertaken and analyzed on a case-by-case basis".

US laws establish right to Speak Anonymously on the Internet and also right to Read Anonymously on the Internet ensuring the principle of free internet ideological confrontation and the right to free movement of information.

"People are permitted to interact pseudonymously and anonymously with each other so long as those acts are not in violation of the law. This ability to speak one's mind without the burden of the other party knowing all the facts about one's identity can foster open communication and robust debate."

The technological developments of recent years caused high attention to the legal and technological possibility to maintain the on line anonymity especially in the face of the multiplication of resources internet monitoring.

The right to internet anonymity is also covered by European legislation that recognizes the fundamental right to data protection, freedom of expression, and freedom of impression. **The European Union Charter of Fundamental Rights recognizes in Article. 8 (Title II: "Freedoms")** the right of everyone to protection of personal data concerning him.

The right to privacy is now essentially the individual's right to have and to maintain control over information about him.

It may be helpful to abolish the anonymity?

In most cases not. The offenses do not become more serious for the mere fact of being committed or planned online, and therefore, there seems no real need to violate the right to anonymity online.

Is a Tor Relay LEGAL in the U.S.

Is running ToR-software client side or a ToR-relay network Legal? In the United States a federal law Title *"17 of the US code 17 USC 512(a)"*,called: *Limitation on Liability relating to materials Online*, states that *"A service provider shall not be liable ... for infringement of copyright"*.

This applies to the -Transitory Digital Network Communication - what this all spells out is that the ToR network is not illegal or any ToR-Relay is also legal and as such under the law you as a U.S citizen are not doing anything illegal when you use ToR -.onion network.

The law establishes that the technological tool isn't not responsible for the crime, but its improper usage represents the crime, whose responsibility it of the person that commits the offense.

Limitations on liability relating to material online

17 USC 512(a) (part of the DMCA) says:

A service provider shall not be liable ... for infringement of copyright by reason of the provider's transmitting, routing, or providing connections for, material through a system ... operated by or for the service provider, or by reason of the intermediate and transient storage of that material in the course of such transmitting, routing, or providing connections, if --the transmission of the material was initiated by or at the direction of a person other than the service provider; the transmission ... is carried out through an automatic technical process without selection of the material by the service provider; the service provider does not select the recipients of the material except as an automatic response to the request of another person; no copy of the material made ... is maintained ... in a manner ordinarily accessible to anyone other than anticipated recipients [or] for a longer period than is reasonably necessary for the transmission...the material is transmitted ...

without modification of its content.512(b) extends the immunity to "generally accepted industry standard" caching.(The DMCA takedown notice procedures you may have heard of are part of 512(c) and only apply to services that store copies of material.)

References:

Copyright Law of the United States of America and Related Laws Contained in Title 17 of the United States

Codehttp://www.copyright.gov/title17/92chap5.html#512

Governments Use of the Deep Dark Web

Government Use

CIA, FBI, NSA, different agencies for an unique intent…global monitoring

We have discussed several times regarding the intention of the **FBI** to create a special unit for internet **monitoring** and surveillance, a task force established to prevent and fight cyber crimes .In reality the Bureau already has different internal units that work with the same purpose and in the last years has promoted different projects for the development of tools and applications for the web monitoring.
The FBI has recently created a secret surveillance unit to project and develop technologic tools and software for Internet and wireless communications monitoring.
FBI is considered one of the most active agencies in this sense, in the last months it has publicly requested the design of a real time monitor for **social networks** that have to be able to identify suspect behaviors that could be interpreted as indicator of presence for an ongoing crime.
The FBI has been lobbying top internet companies like Yahoo and Google to support a proposal that would force them to provide backdoors for government surveillance, according to CNET. The purpose of the collaboration between FBI and major IT companies and Internet services providers is tied to the will of the agency to arrive at the definition of legislation that allows law enforcement to have the controversial backdoor.
FBI desires the collaboration of the major player of the IT sector to implement specific backdoor stubs inside their products with intent to make them wiretap-friendly, the request is related to all those communication platforms, social network, email providers, chats and instant messaging.

The FBI has trying to maintain maximum reserve on the Unit called the Domestic Communications Assistance Center, for which the Senate committee has already allocated $54 million assigning to it the mission to create technologies for law enforcement to intercept and analyze communications data.

The power conferred to the unit is wide, every single communication through social networks and over internet in general should be intercepted by the hardware platforms and software applications that the unit have to implement.

In February 2011, CNET reported that then-FBI general counsel Valerie Caproni was planning to warn Congress of what the bureau calls its **"Going Dark"** problem, illustrating how the wiretapping capabilities were being reduced with the progress of technology.

Caproni singled out "Web-based e-mail, social-networking sites, and peer-to-peer communications" as problems that have left the FBI "increasingly unable" to conduct the same kind of wiretapping it could in the past.

"Going Dark" is the FBI's codename for its project to extend its ability to real time wiretap communications, it is born inside the bureau, employing 107 full-time expert starting from 2009.

According the declaration of Electronic Frontier Foundation attorney Kevin Bankston FBI already can intercept messages on social-networking sites and Web-based e-mail services, the system used is known as Carnivore, later renamed DCS1000. The interception is possible because Facebook messages and Gmail messages travel in plain text over those same broadband wires for which the FBI demanded wiretapping capability.

The main problem is related to rapid technological evolutions that make obsolescent surveillance systems in short time, due this reason the request of FBI to include a backdoor in any products that could be involved in communication, like social networking and also online **games consoles**.

The Domestic Communications Assistance Center represents the technological factory of the "Going Dark" project for the internet wiretapping, the **document**, FY 2013

Performance Budget Congressional Submission refers to the recent establishment of DCAC:
While progress is expected through DEA's participation in the recently established Department-wide Domestic Communications Assistance Center (DCAC) led by the FBI to address the growing technological gap between law enforcement's electronic surveillance capabilities and the number and variety of communications devices available to the public, the foremost challenge confronting U.S. law enforcement is the diminishing ability to conduct lawful electronic intercepts on current and emerging communications technologies as communications providers continue to offer new and improved services and features to customers. Addressing this issue is critical to maintain law enforcement's ability to conduct lawful criminal intercepts.
The position of the US authorities is worrying, they want to impose to every internet service provider to give full access to Government for surveillance purpose, according the amendment to CALEA, the Communications Assistance for Law Enforcement Act.
Contrary to what one might think about the news there is no noise, no political debate, confirming a will that seems a common intent.
To confirm that the FBI is allocating new skilled personnel to the unit a job announcement for the DCAC has been published with a deadline of May 2. Analyzing the announcement we can have an idea on the technological skills requested, such as a meaningful experience with "electronic surveillance standards" including PacketCable, QChat and T1.678 (VoIP communications). One required skill for the position, which pays up to $136,771 a year, is evaluating "electronic surveillance solutions" for "emerging" technologies.

Declan McCullagh, chief political correspondent for CNET, in an **excellent** article on the argument has reported:
The NDCAC will have the functionality to leverage the research and development efforts of federal, state, and local law enforcement with respect to electronic surveillance

capabilities and facilitate the sharing of technology among law enforcement agencies. Technical personnel from other federal, state, and local law enforcement agencies will be able to obtain advice and guidance if they have difficulty in attempting to implement lawful electronic surveillance court orders.

It is important to point out that the NDCAC will not be responsible for the actual execution of any electronic surveillance court orders and will not have any direct operational or investigative role in investigations. It will provide the technical knowledge and referrals in response to law enforcement's requests for technical assistance.

The project is really ambitious and without doubt it will involve all the main intelligence agencies of the country, such as Drug Enforcement Administration and National Security Agency.

NSA also is massive investing in monitoring technology, a couple of months ago we have learned that the agency is building the country's biggest Spy Center in the little known city of Bluffdale. The center, named Utah Data Center is under construction by contractors with top-secret clearances.

Its purpose is to intercept, decipher, and analyze every world's communications under investigation using every kind of transmission. The center will have a final cost of $2 billion and should be operative in September 2013. Its databases will be store all forms of communication, including the complete private emails, cell phone calls, search engine researches and every kind of digital data related to every individual. The imperative is to monitor everything!

It's clear the dimension of the project that has the purpose to cover monitoring need of every type including of course satellite communication, phone calls, computer data and geostationary satellite data.

The Deep Dark Web – the hidden web

Once the Data Center it's operational it will be fed data collected by the agency's eavesdropping satellites, overseas listening posts, and secret monitoring rooms in telecom facilities throughout the US.

Federal Bureau Of Investigation

Job Title: IT Specialist (National Domestic Communications Assistance Center-NDCAC) GS 13/14/ (FBI)
Department: Department Of Justice
Agency: Federal Bureau of Investigation
Job Announcement Number: 18-2012-0062

SALARY RANGE:	$89,033.00 to $135,771.00 / Per Year
OPEN PERIOD:	Thursday, April 26, 2012 to Wednesday, May 02, 2012
SERIES & GRADE:	GS-2210-13/14
POSITION INFORMATION:	* - Permanent/Full-Time
PROMOTION POTENTIAL:	14
DUTY LOCATIONS:	2 vacancy(s) - Quantico, VA, US View Map
WHO MAY BE CONSIDERED:	Open to current FBI employees in all locations.

This position is being advertised concurrently with Announcement Number 18-2012-0061. Candidates who wish to be considered on External and FBI only certificates must apply to both announcements.

Applications will not be accepted from outside the area of consideration.

DUTIES: Back to top

GS 13:

- Develops and maintains technical investigative IT systems supporting helpdesk, technology sharing, training, standards development, solution verification and database management operations.
- Provides informational assistance, coordination and technical guidance to state, local and other federal law enforcement (LE) organizations.
- Ensures the integrity, standardization, and accessibility of programmatic data.
- Monitors contractor efforts in developing, maintaining and enhancing computer application software.
- Interacts effectively with LE personnel, management, co-workers and the communications industry to ensure that work performed correlates to defined objectives.

GS 14:

- Manages technical investigative IT systems supporting helpdesk, technology sharing, training, standards development, solution verification and database management operations.
- Provides informational assistance, coordination and technical guidance to lower grade ITS personnel, state, local and other federal law enforcement (LE) organizations.
- Responsible for the security, integrity, standardization, policy compliance and accessibility of programmatic data.
- Oversees contractor efforts in developing, maintaining and enhancing computer applications software.
- Interacts effectively with LE personnel, the communications industry and others to meet immediate and long-term customer satisfaction and other operational objectives.

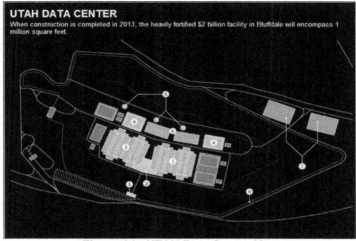

Figure 34 - UTAH Data Center Map

All that data will then be accessible to the NSA's code breakers, data-miners, China analysts, counterterrorism specialists, and others working at its Fort Meade headquarters and around

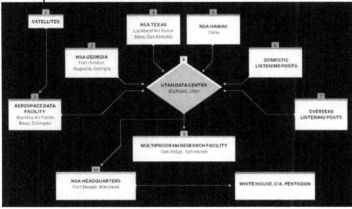

Figure 35 - NSA Spying Architecture

the world.

Someone has defined the project as the NSA monitoring cloud

The information I'm proposing should not deceive, in reality the country is already littered with centers for the analysis of data traffic and phone interception that make use of sophisticated software programs that conduct "deep packet inspection," examining Internet traffic as it passes through the 10-gigabit-per-second cables at the speed of light. One of the main software has been developed by company called **Narus** and is controlled remotely from NSA headquarters at Fort Meade in Maryland. Any suspicion communication is automatically recorded and transmitted to the NSA for further analysis.

Also other agency are interested to monitoring and surveillance, let's introduce project sponsored by CIA, the intelligence agency is now interested to gather information from every intelligent devices that is surrounding us to spy on every US citizen. We have introduced months ago a spying project that has the intent to acquire information from gaming platform all over the world, a mine of data to collect and analyze.

Let's me conclude the article speaking of the most interesting part of the web, the one define **Deep Web**, that every agency is infiltrating, a volume of data impressive if compared to the ordinary web. the Deep Web represent today a mine of information with high level of interest, this invisible portion of web is considered in fact the homeland for cybercrime, intelligence agencies and Hacktivist, due this reason it is considered fundamental to be able to control this controversial cyber scenario.

In the Deep Web are hidden protected data, government communications and noncommercial file-sharing between trusted peers.

"The deep web contains government reports, databases, and other sources of information of high value to DOD and the intelligence community," according to a 2010 Defense Science Board report.

"Alternative tools are needed to find and index data in the deep web … Stealing the classified secrets of a potential adversary is where the [intelligence] community is most comfortable."
It 'clear that the huge investments mentioned are
a blatant invasion of privacy in the name of security, but the scope of the projects suggests that no law or constitution can oppose.
What will invent the human intellect to escape
this modern form of control?

Government & Tor Network

In the last years the Deep Web has reached an impressive size, to give an idea of the growth let's remind that one of the foremost authorities on the topic, Michael K Bergman, in the late 90s he undertook research that proved a dimension two or three times bigger than the regular web. Ten years later in 2001 he published a paper on the deep web that is still regularly cited today where he declaring that "The deep web was 400 to 550 times larger than the commonly defined world wide web,", an impressive progression, we can hazard that the hidden web is the fastest growing category on the internet, an immeasurable quantity of information of any kind.

Another decade is passed from that assertion and we can imagine what could be the actual ratio between the dimension of the clear web and the Deep Web,

Governments are conscious of the potentiality of this mine of data and have massively invested in research on the topic with the intent to find an efficient process to analyze the data trying to explore that component of internet hidden to the search engines.

But why a government could be interested to the control of Deep Web?

There are several reasons to justify the effort spent by governments and government agencies on the usage of Deep Web, in a first classification we can think to:

Monitoring – Of course the primary purpose is the exercise of monitoring, intelligence agencies and cyber commands spend a lot of time and involve high skilled resources trying to infiltrate the network searching for sensible documentation and capturing the sentiment of the internet users. We have already demonstrated how much useful could be the analysis of the deep web usage to prevent censorship phenomena. Many researches have been financed by governments for the development of automated spider with the hope to try to map the hidden networks identified resources and their users, but there are a lot of technical limitation that still avoid the identification of entities in the Deep Web.

Control – Of course monitoring activities are just a form of supervision of the hidden web, it gives to governments a picture of the state of the art of several phenomenon such as cybercrime and hacktivism. The study of hidden web is a fundamental component for governments to guarantee homeland security and to analyze movements that could harm national security. Often the monitoring is just the prelude to actions of censorship and repression against dissents and opponent to the regime. In many parts of the words governments afraid the organization of movements of opposition to the regime, due this reason they implement systems able to deep inspect traffic recognizing the patterns related to the principal anonymization networks such us Tor. These systems are able to deep inspect packets making possible internet closure to common people for politic reason.

In recent years we have observed the scandalous growth of a florid market for digital control and surveillance in which Western companies sell technologies with impunity to authoritarian regimes, enabling them to spy on and suppress any opposition. An estimated annual turnover of five billion dollars that must induce serious reflection.

It's clear that in similar context individuals that fight for their right adopt any precaution to masquerade their real identity to protect their life. This control market is an old story, the question that we must raise to our society is:

How much is a human life? Are we really able to sell it in the name of money?

Emblematic the response provided by a statement of Microsoft researcher Danah Boyd:

"Most companies will say publicly that they are doing everything possible to protect citizens when in fact they are doing endless concessions and taking policy decisions that will eventually damage them."

Document sharing – that is a typical usage of Deep Web made my agents under coverage that operate in hostile areas and that using hidden services of various nature are able to share document and information with their references or to masses of people such as organizations. Again hidden web represents the optimum compromise between anonymity and connectivity.

Many people use the Tor network to surf anonymously and protect their privacy, let's consider how much is dangerous internet for many people located in countries such China, Iran and Syria today. Despite Tor network is an efficient network able to preserve user identity it must be kept in serious consideration the power of traffic analysis, critical instants during Tor usage is the entry in the network that could be easy traced. The main cyber threat for Tor users is represented by the government infiltration, group of expert analysts and hacker state-sponsored daily work searching for services and resources related to "cases" of interest. The governments agents work silently for years building their hidden reputation taking care of their fake identities for which they try to increase the reputation. With similar techniques are build up fake services to attract victims and try to discover their identities, the deep web for example has been used in many cases as the cyber scenario for malware spread especially for cyber espionage operations.

Recently the FBI and DEA had been directed to investigate Tor networks, and specifically the Silk Road marketplace infiltrating its agents in similar way they usually do with other anonymous Tor marketplaces.
On April 2012, Federal, state, and international law enforcement authorities have arrested eight people who are accused of drug trafficking and money laundering operating in the deep web with on-line narcotics market place "The Farmer's Market". The marketplace which sold a variety of

controlled substances to approximately 3,000 customers in 34 countries and 50 states.

It must be considered that in the last decade we have observed the raise of cyber attacks, no matter their purpose, cyber warfare or cyber espionage for military or private business, they have demonstrated how much dangerous is a cyber offensive.

The U.S.'s leading cyber warrior has estimated that private businesses are losing hundreds of billions to cyber espionage and cybercrimes, and the total expense to prevents those phenomena is increasing making companies less competitive in the causes of costs.

The main problem is to address this cyber threats with an appropriate cyber strategy first and after involving capable experts, and cyber threat also passes through the deep web that provide an excellent environment to operate in anonymity.

The question is continuously debated by the US high officials, four-star Gen. Keith Alexander, director of the secretive National Security Agency and head of the Pentagon's Cyber Command, declared recently that the illicit cyberspace activities essentially amounted to "the greatest transfer of wealth in history."

The general alerted the US Government on an imminent dangerous for the national security, in a recent public intervention he said U.S. companies lose $250 billion to intellectual property theft every year.

The high official referred of data
from Symantec and McAfee reports that show an alarming scenario, $114 billion was lost only due cybercrime activities, and the number could be as high as $388 billion if the value of time and business opportunities lost is included. In particular McAfee firm proposed worst data, today $1 trillion is spent globally in remediation.

Which are the main cyber threat that are arming governments?

Malware and botnets represent the great challenge to security, according McAfee 75 million unique pieces of

malware have been detected since now in their database, an amazing figure if we consider the related damage.
Same concerns regarding the botnets and their diffusion, we are assisting to an evolution of the technology adopted, let's introduce for example the Peer-to-Peer based botnet, and the mechanism used for their diffusion.
Many concerns are also related to the business model, malware as service or C2C, adopted by cybercrime that make possible the creation of botnet also for not experts.
Cybercrime is not only the unique concern of US Government, we must take in care of the increasing adoption of cyber operations made by foreign governments and also the hacktivism phenomenon. Both are cyber threats, both could compromise national security, both could expose sensible information. Dedicated chapter must be reserved for critical infrastructures, according the last ICS-CERT report the number of attacks is passed form 9 in 2009 to more than 160 in 2011, and the trend demonstrate a constant growth.
In the described scenario it's is to recognize the importance to monitor and infiltrate the Deep Web, the cyberspace that host major number of host and services that criminals and foreign governments could use to prepare or conduct a cyber attack.

Infiltrate or block- that is the question!
It's known the origin of Tor, the project comes from a secret protocol of US navy, back in the 90's, using a multiplayer approach it allows to masquerade the user's IP address, due this reason a growing number of surfers is using it to remain hidden to eye of governments and the web's giants.
The project was after released to the open research community of *Electronic Frontier Foundation* (EFF) that has continued the development and its divulgation, but the real question is why US Corp has worked to a special project making it public.

A diffused theory consider the project an aggregator for "interesting content" that could be subject to analysis, through the promise of anonymity it possible to attract politicians, dissident, Hacktivist and cyber criminal in the same space, the cyber space. It's common opinion the US Government, but also other entities, are involving groups of hackers to collect and analyze data to perform governments research.

In many cases it has been hypothesized that the groups of US volunteers, participating to Project Vigilant has also infiltrated TOR networks. The group is responsible for tracking of more that 250 million IP addresses a day providing detailed analysis of intercepted traffic.

The group is considered as secret government contractor responsible for the monitoring traffic of 12 regional Internet Service Providers, thanks to its researches they traced the source of a video, named "Collateral Murder", published by Wikileaks showing a U.S. Apache helicopter killing several civilians and two journalists in a suburb of Baghdad The group was also responsible of the identification of Bradley Manning to the authorities.

Chet Uber, the director of Fort Pierce, Fl.-based Project Vigilant, declared that ISP monitoring is just one form of intelligence that Vigilant volunteers , the groups implements open source intelligence, in Iran, for example, Vigilant created an anonymous Internet proxy service to give voice to the local dissidents.

To ensure an anonymous communication, the data transferred via the Tor network must pass through at least three different entities, the origin of the communications known as the "entry router", the destination communications known as the "output router" and one or more intermediate nodes.

The attack on the Tor network by governments, has moved substantially in two directions, from a legal and technological.

Because of the abuse seen in the network of resources, government representatives argue that each output node should be held responsible for the traffic it carries, to limit all forms of crime.
Obviously such an approach would undermine the very concept of anonymous network.

In terms of technology, as discussed above, some control can be carried out by analyzing the incoming traffic to entry servers that inevitably know the user's IP before it leaves lose its tracks in the deep web. This is a weak point, the users must make sure that they connect to a node without bad intentions, for this reason Tor has introduced a series of official lists to provide a list of Tor "trusted" nodes.

Instead of legislating on the legality of the Tor network, some governments are inclined to infiltrate it with undercover agents and providing services to monitor traffic. The outgoing traffic from each exit node cannot be encrypted to avoid reception to the destination server, for this reason the use of insecure protocols like POP, IMAP and FTP may allow the identification of sensitive user data such as their credentials.

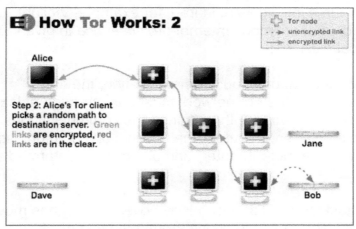

Figure 36 - Tor Routing

There are therefore risks that they must be properly dealt with, the use of an unprotected external application could allow the tracking of the 'user's IP.

Example of attack to Tor network

An attack technically possible is the classic "man in the middle" where a node can intercept or modify the contents of packets traveling through it. According to some experts, the technique was used by Wikileaks activists to obtain confidential information.

The exit node are precious source of information on the overall traffic of Tor networks, they represent the last of each connection and the packet from the TOR client is decrypted to be sent to the final destination. As we have introduced in this phase is possible to conduct traffic analysis detecting any illegal and unethical activities such as a spam campaign or the transfer of child porno material.

But TOR protocol does not provide end-to-end encryption making possible to sniff unencrypted
protocols such as HTTP, POP or SMTP on TOR exit nodes. Users are usually convinced that Tor is able to grant total anonymity ignoring the fact that intercepting information on exit nodes is also possible to reveal its identity.
In this phase is possible to intercept useful traffic containing credential to web site or also other sensible info.

Another fundamental consideration is that on an exit node it is possible to inject any kind of content that will be considered legitimate by destination client that is not able to check the integrity of transmission protocol used.

The analysis of traffic could also provide other useful information regarding the usage of the TOR net network, examining for example the User-Agent tag in HTTP traffic (destination port 80), it's possible to discover the OS system used and browser version, a useful data in case someone is interested to package an APT attacks targeting specific platforms.

Compromise the TOR Anonymity

The great question is "Is it possible to discover user's IP address?", well unfortunately the response is "yes, under specific conditions".

Let me enumerate some procedure described in literature:

- Of course from an ISP perspective analyzing large quantity of TOR traffic, namely on the first and the last node, and applying statistical analysis, it is possible to discover the source of a connection.
- Is it possible to determine the identity of a user on a web server or on an exit node (since the biggest amount of traffic was unencrypted HTTP)? Yes it's possible thank incorrect configurations of applications on TOR client, let's think for example to a miss-configured browser plug-in that could reveals client IP, either through HTTP or even with raw sockets (TCP or UDP).
- DNS Leak, TOR can be used as a SOCKS proxy and can be used for any TCP connection, but consider that the requests are sent differently to SOCKS proxy according the SOCKS versions used. With SOCKS 4 and mostly also with SOCKS 5 requests, the target host is given with its IP address and not by its FQDN. This implies that the browser makes his own DNS requests to resolve the FQDN the user entered to an IP address which can then be sent to the SOCKS proxy (TOR).
  "When the application uses SOCKS 4 or SOCKS 5 to give Tor an IP address, Tor guesses that it 'probably' got the IP address non-anonymously from a DNS server. That's why it gives you a warning message: you probably aren't as anonymous as you think."

The Tor Project Blog suggest the following action to avoid problems:

For HTTP (web browsing), either configure your browser to perform remote DNS lookups or use a socks4a-capable HTTP proxy, such as Polipo. For instant messaging or IRC, use Gaim or XChat. For other programs, consider using freecap (on Win32) or dsocks (on BSD). You can use TorDNS as a local DNS server to rectify the DNS leakage.

- User's identity could also be revealed setting a persistent cookie on the client browser, in this way a user could be tracked over various requests. To avoid that these cookies are sent back to the server it's necessary to use tools such as Privoxy tool.
- Updates During Tor could expose user's identity, especially for updated that refers not SSL-enabled websites. It is possible for malicious Tor nodes to hijack these applications and replace them with malicious ones. Typical example it provided by existing browser extensions.
- Another possible font of problem for user's identity is related to the navigation on specific web site, such as YouTube, that require third party browser plug-in such as Flash. These plug-in operate independently from Firefox and can perform actions that compromise the anonymity, for example querying user local IP address, or storing their own cookies. Let's note that how declared in TOR project that:
The Tor Browser Bundle does not work with Flash or other plug-in by design. If you wish to run these plug-in over Tor, you need to install Tor and configure your own instance of Firefox.

TOR network is a precious resource to guarantee user anonymity, but we must consider that despite the implicit security of the protocol the overall attack surface is large. When we examine the user's iteration we must consider all the components involved in the process, we have learnt that between browser and remote web server it's possible to exploit the vulnerabilities of several components such as browser plug-in.

Due the exposed reasons it's important to access TOR network with few precautions:

- Use an isolated environment running web browser and Tor inside a virtual machine. A good alternative is the use of LiveCD solution such as or The Amnesic Incognito Live System that creates a secure, transparent proxy to protect you from proxy bypass, however issues with local IP address discovery and Flash cookies still remain.
- Limit the installed software to the strictly necessary.
- Create a restrictive egress firewall
- Don't trust content that was downloaded over unencrypted channels.

Always remind that nothing is totally secure and that in many cases human factor can poses serious risks to the user's identity and its anonymity.

Dear Tor Mail User –government intervention
Early this morning, April 20, 2012 our domain registrar nic.ru suspended the domain tormail.net. The reason they gave is because they require us to submit ID documents to them, apostatized and certified by the Russian Embassy. We are unable to do this to protect our own identity, and also this request is very unusual and suspicious. They have further refused to unlock the domain and allow us to transfer it to a different registrar.

We have filed a complaint with ICANN as per the domain transfer rules, they are not allowed to do this. As it is the weekend, we probably wont get a response until next week, and even to transfer a domain normally takes about a week to be completed. For this reason, at the earliest we can hope for is to have the domain back within two weeks. It is possible the domain is gone for good and it may not be possible to get it back.

Up until two months ago, the domain was registered with a USA company, Moniker domains. They were great and we had no problems with them, but with the recent domain seizures we decided to move the domain offshore. It appears this was a big mistake, the Russian providers are much worse!
The chances of getting the domain back does not look good, and even if we get it back it will take a long time. For that reason we have registered a new domain name tormail.org and will use that one to continue the service. If we do get the tormail.net domain back, we will change back to using that one.
Every user who had a @tormail.net address now has the same address @tormail.org Your new email address is:
http://jhiwjjlqpyawmpjx.onion/

Sorry for the inconvenience, but we were taken by surprise by this and had no time to avoid it. --Admin.

The Business Side of the Deep Dark Web -

The Black Market

Tor Black Market Cybercrime Ecosystem

The Black Market in cyber space exist in both the surface-Web and the dark-Web. For some reason the basic Internet user thinks the ToR-.onion network is for bad guys only but it's completely wrong. The Black Market is only a small part of the immense DeepWeb but concepts of anonymity and cyber crimes generate in the collective imaginary wrong perception of a common place where it is possible to make business. The general concession is the black market rules in ToR onion-Land is a joke, let see why.

What is the Cyber Black Market?
A **black market** or **underground economy** is a market in goods or services, which operates outside the formal one(s) supported by established state power. Cybercrime is

considered by Department of Homeland Security (DHS) a bigger threat than terrorism and following a list of key figure on the phenomenon provided by Symantec/Norton related the Cyber Crime **in the Surface-Web:**

- Cybercrime cost $388 billion across 24 countries.
- 69% of adults have been a victim of cybercrime.
- 10% of mobile phone users have experienced cybercrime, up 42% from last year.
- Cybercrime costs the world significantly more than the global black market in marijuana, cocaine and heroin combined ($288B).
- Increasing of what is considered as "White Collar - Cyber Crime"

Figure 37 - Symantec CyberCrime Report 2011

Blue Collar -Cyber Crime

Now take the ToR-.onion Black Market: It's a little more in your face drugs, guns, stolen goods, sex, hacked data- all in the dark-Web you know that these merchants are crooks and criminals. In Silk Road or Black Market Reload they now verified sellers and now even buyers in an attempt to legit. A trust relationship for crooks, is really funny, what does verified mean in these .onion market-places?
It usually mean that the admin of the site has somehow check that this is a real person real whatever. or he has done business with someone and they write a nice review. Never thinking that the review could be the crook with another login name just like they do in the surface-Web.

Imagine a user that would not do business with any black market in the surface-Web or the dark-Web -If his products are bad at least he can complain to Amazon when he do business whit them, he can't do anything but writes a bad review in "Black Market-Reload" in the dark-Web.
  -honest crooks? Yeah give me a break..

At least In the Tor-.onion Black Market you can assume everyone is a thief, a crook or a criminal. In the clear-web you don't know who to trust … this is a subtle but very important consideration to make.

Cybercrime Ecosystem.

Let's look at the black market in the surface web.:

WHITE COLLAR CYBER CRIMES – **cybercrime ecosystem**
ATM skimming: – ATM skimming is proliferating, next to the overall availability of bank plastic cards, holograms and pretty much everything a carder needs to cash out the fraudulently obtained credit card data.

Pharmaceutical e-mail spam problem: -The general public is addictive to drugs- legal – illegal – copy-drugs – fake claim drugs – and they e-mail you the consumer you seen them "Viagra" cheap -Canada – Europe – nah it from Asia or Russia.

Eastern Europe is the epicenter of the cybercrime epidemic-financially-motivated cybercrime – without question hackers in Russia and Eastern Europe are the most active, if not also the most profitable. Sophisticated groups tend to be regional and stick to attacking their own, Brazil is a good example.

Active malware/crimeware campaigns:
Sophisticated cybercriminals:

Risk-forwarding cybercrime ecosystem
the rise of money mule recruitment are reshipping mules more popular than money mules advanced persistent threats (APT attacks)

Let's look at the black market in the dark web.:
The most interesting goods to exchange and of interest are BLUE/BROWN/BLACK-(low end) COLLAR CYBER CRIMES such as:

- Selling Drugs
- Selling Guns and explosives
- Selling Stolen goods
- Selling Hacked Data
- Selling Sex
- Buy an Assassin
- Rent a Hacker

So now we can see that in the Surface black market the legit merchants are watching everything you do and selling your information to the highest bidder. While the **sophisticated crimes** against normal people backed by organized crimes is normal in the clear-Web. In the Deep -Dark -Tor -.onion web the **low-end criminals** haunt this area.

The problem I have is that the same things that are in the deep dark web are the same things I can get at -*EBAy*- Guns – Stolen Goods, -*CraigsList*- Assassin, legal/illegal Drugs, Sex, Stolen Damage Goods and Drugs, so in the surface web you can get the same as the dark web, so what's the difference??
At least inside the matrix you have more anonymity –

No matter the anonymity, we would not do business with the black market in the deep web or out, use your own common sense my friends. We are judging that those people that use the ToR protocol to communicate with more privacy are all bad when only a few sites sell (bad) stuff there is some good in the network – and – *bottom line* –it's all about freedom of choice.
The other thing is that the commercial cyber criminals ecosystem in the clear-Web has not picked up on this newer technology (ToR-onion network) that is more secure and are harder to scam and gain your personal and their information while online.

Tor hides communication patterns by relaying data through volunteer servers

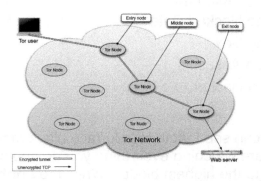

Diagram: Robert Watson

Figure 38 - Tor Network

The Black Market is the same or worse in the surface web than in the deep-dark web so- stay away from the black market period use the ToR network to be smarter, without leaving digital breadcrumbs -

Below there are our notes and the ToR Cleaned Hidden Directory Wiki so you can see yourself some of the things that go into the black market Tor-.onion network- Remember that this is only a small part of the network, there are millions of terabytes undiscovered in the ToR-.onion network, it's just hidden because they don't want you know.

George Carlin *said*:
it best – *You are not in the club- and they are not going to let you in – they are never going to let you in- you're screwed...!*

They are going to scare you away from the ToR-.onion network because "they" desire to hide their little business secrets in this network and they what silence around.
We have found a great article from "Kerb on Security Interview" outlining the cyber criminal ecosystem where we drew a lot of the surface web black market anyway.

The Digital Economy -xxx

Cyber Black Market- Underground Economy

We read that the FBI leaked an unclassified report on 24 April 2012 Intelligence Assessment *"BitCoin Virtual Currency: (Unique Features Present Distinct Challenges for Deterring Illicit Activity"* :

http://cryptome.org/2012/05/fbi-bitcoin.pdf

At that time BitCoins (BTC) were going about **$4.25 USD** 05/2012 per coin -- as of **Sun: Jun17 2012** it trading at **$6:26714 a high of $6.52999 and low of $6.22130** check out the currency value trend on https://mtgox.com/ and expected to go up to *$20-25 USD by Christmas 2012, we don't think so!!!*

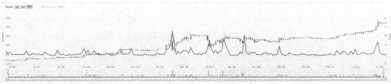

Figure 39 - MTGox - Currency Trend - July 2012

All that glitters is not-gold – with BitCoins *mAyBe -sl -nO –*

Digital Currency -basics

One of the most talked about NEW currency is- **"Bitcoin"** Let me tell you about them first - By using proven strong cryptography, a new currency has been created for the internet. One of the key features of Bitcoin is that it is an open system with no person or authority that governs the system. This means that you can treat it like cash: nobody can freeze your account, no chargeback's, complete transparency and more.

These are some other e-currencies-

Perfect Money – Liberty Reserves -Wire Transfer - Pecunix -HD-Money -C-Gold -VouchX -Cosmic Pay - MtGox Coupons -Boleto -Banco Rendimento -CyberPlat -Qiwi -Money Gram -CVS ?7-11 -Wal-Mart -BitStamps - Dwolla -BTC-E Coupons and 7/11 moneyPaks.

Today (Bitcoins-BTC) and other digital currencies are only "chump change" but it's getting big enough that the FBI leaked a report about (Bitcoins-BTC) - by the way BTC have only been around since 2009 – 3 years ago there were no BTC and today the FBI is leaking reports not how bad they are. The report claims cyber criminals use BTC for money laundry, but in the same report the FBI tell us how to safely use BTC so they are untraceable. We don't get it… Why would they leak this unless they already have a backdoor to the laundry of BTC. The key to BTC is "blockchain" you must understand is that the blockchain of a BTC job to record every transaction, and report it to the peer to peer network so everyone knows the transaction –then a laundry service strips away this from the blockchain – more testing need to be done on this—Another way to laundry is to get your money back with someone else's money this would clean your digital signature, but what if their fingerprint is even more dirty that yours and your new Bitcoins come from stolen account or somewhere else- but more research need to be done into BTC…. Bitcoin laundry service is being recommended by the FBI – once again we don't get it folks – --/ beware Bill Robinson –beware /--

Now the other part is that if the FBI is getting interested in Bitcoins(BTC) then the "evil bankers" are getting into this new digital currency deal, come on untraceable currency – a bankers dream… these money traders will take a look at (Bitcoins-BTC) and once they get a whiff of the virtual money they will strike. Commercial criminals are already doing it, why not the bankers – same difference.

The Chart below was in Early June, today July 21 Bitcoins
are at $8.91 USD
(http://bitcoincharts.com/markets/currencies/)

Currencies

Currency	24h	7 days	30 days
AUD	6.40	6.00	5.57
BRL	14.00	14.09	12.15
CAD	6.30	5.76	5.34
CHF	--	--	5.12
CNY	39.77	37.15	34.34
DKK	--	33.00	33.53
EUR	5.23	4.81	4.40
GBP	4.18	3.88	3.55
HKD	--	--	40.20
JPY	518.51	496.13	450.08
NZD	--	7.06	6.86
PLN	21.55	20.23	18.44
RUB	205.89	205.18	180.00
SEK	51.13	42.90	41.33
SGD	--	--	6.74
SLL	1855.82	1641.44	1444.84
THB	--	192.36	192.32
USD	6.34	5.96	5.47

Figure 40 – Currencies prices for 1 BITCOIN

As you can see from BTC Trend while currencies from all
over the world are going down because of the current
financial world problems, austerity and in some EU countries
BitCoins are going UP.
Ever heard of Hal-Cash – from Russia with Love—It's being
marketed in South America as the new digital currency –
Market to Latin America—

Anon Visa Debit Card, load with PP, LR, BTC and IBAN! Selling 100% valid CVV & dumps - Verified Vendor, rottenjubjub
(UPDATED) Visa Debit Card with IBAN, 4 currencies, Lowest Prices! Unlimited Stealth Paypal Accounts and How to Withdraw
-= US Bank Accounts =- -= Now $ Hiring =- -= Drops Shipping =- -= Exclusive Services =- -= Cashout =-
US CC + Worldwide CC, Cheapest US/CAN FULLS! Always Valid Guaranteed!! US Online Bank account creation and cashout Guide!

Figure 41 - Scams selling Visa cards for USD cash

In the previous figure is an add from the deep web that is
selling 100% anon visa cards with loaded BitCoins or
whatever currency you want on them – by the way they are
looking for unemployed greedy people for money mules --

Figure 42 Bitcoins and other fiat currencies

and Drop Shipments mule scams for any sucker that want this kind of job- you are a fool to buy this our opinion they can sell you loaded Visa Card on one hand and Selling 100% Valid CVV and dumps of these card we assume but we are a paranoids – we may be wrong – don't try this at home kiddies—//

BitCoins are coming up and they are replacing the new fiat currencies especially in EU because of the current problems in Greece and Spain. Below we added a list of -**[1]Ways to get bitCoins,** As you can see if you go to these they are scams for Gambling and all kinds of underworld stuff, but how many people play Online Poker and other gambling games?
Oh and these are all in the ClearWeb, yes the evil Internet not the ToR-.onion network ..

Now the funny part is you can go to 7-11, Wal-Mart and just about any place and buy into this new currency so it's not illegal to use these currencies, maybe we are the only stupid that don't use this currency, but many, many merchants are now accepting all these new online currencies.
So maybe it's not so stupid If someone wants to buy my-1972 Action GI Joe Doll why shouldn't I let him or her pay in BitCoins or any other currency.

Now in the Black Market of the ToR-.onion network it's alive and well, and now as you can see this is a boom to criminals to laundry their cash.

(
http://clsvtzwzdgzkjda7.onion/viewtopic.php?f=50&t=1803&sid=4e3a4c75f43e3e82fe011d6c1e6601df&start=10)

But consider that criminals been using also FarmVille and other games to laundry money so why not use this new untraceable money? We will leave the crime stuff for anther posting but we just wanted to give you all a taste of what is

going on and what can happened with your money.

Reference: Lab Notes

http://bitcoincharts.com/	BitCoin trend charts
https://mtgox.com/	BitCoin Currencies
http://translate.google.com/ translate?hl=en&sl=&tl=en &u=http%3A%2F%2Fgb.pl %2Fbanki%2Fkarty%2Fwyp lata-z-bankomatu-bez-karty.html	Withdrawals from an ATM without a card
http://www.halcashusa.com /	Hal-Cash global money transfer network

How Does Bitcoin Work?

To use Bitcoin, an individual first downloads and installs the free Bitcoin software (client).
The application uses *Public Key Cryptography* (PKI) to automatically generate a Bitcoin address
where the user can receive payments. The address is a unique 36 character-long string of
numbers and letters and is stored in a user's virtual "wallet" on his or her local file system. Users
can create as many Bitcoin addresses as they like to receive payments and can use a new address
for every transaction they receive.

To send bitCoins, users input the address they would like to send their bitCoins to and the
amount of bitCoins they would like to transfer. The user's computer then digitally signs the
transaction and sends the information to the distributed, P2P Bitcoin network. The P2P network
verifies that the person sending the bitCoins is the current owner of the bitCoins they are sending,
prohibiting a malicious user from spending the same bitCoins twice. Once the transaction has
been validated by the Bitcoin network, receivers can spend the bitCoins they have received. This
process usually takes a few minutes and is not reversible.

Figure 44 -BitCoin Transfer

A fundamental concept is that Bitcoin software program controls the rate of BitCoin creation, but it does not control the market value of a BitCoin that is determined by the supply of bitCoins in circulation
and people's desire to hold or trade bitCoins. Unlike most fiat currencies, in which central banks can arbitrarily increase the supply of currency, Bitcoin is designed to eventually contain million bitCoins; no additional coins will be created after that point, preventing inflation. Bitcoin was created in such a way that the clients "mine" bitCoins at a predetermined rate.
This following chart illustrates the growth rate from 2009 to 2033, the year the last new BitCoin will be created.

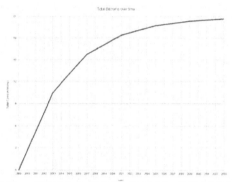

Total Bitcoins over time

BEWARE – REAL LINKS REAL SCAMS
[1]Ways to get bitCoins   ClearWeb Sites not ToR- onion
network stuff – this is th
about the new scam to make him/her a cool million.

Figure 45 - Total Bitcoins over time

http://bit.ly/cmpbx (**exchange**) https://campbx.com/
http://bit.ly/btcxchange (**exchange**)
http://www.cryptoxchange.com/ Australian -Last Price :
6.49999 Buy :6.56200 Sell : 6.56115 Volume : 351.61962
http://bit.ly/virwox1 (**exchange**) https://www.virwox.com/
53,267 users / **15,320,752,995** L$ exchanged
http://bit.ly/coinabul Physical Gold http://coinabul.com/   **BTC
Spot: $6.41 Australia**

http://bit.ly/triplemining (**mining pool**)
https://opticbit.triplemining.com/register -BTC Mining Pool
http://bit.ly/poolcoin (**mining pool**) http://pool.betcoin.co/
http://bit.ly/btcplus (**java cpw web pool**)
http://www.bitcoinplus.com/ BTC Mining Scam
http://bit.ly/mycryptcoin (**free btc**) http://mycryptcoin.com/
http://bit.ly/bitcrate (**free**) http://www.bitcrate.net/
http://bit.ly/btcbonus (**rebates for online purchases**)
http://bitcoinbonus.com/
http://bit.ly/bitgigs (**classified/fiber like**)
http://www.bitgigs.com/ Work or sell for BTC money
http://bit.ly/freebtc1 (**survey**) http://www.freebitcoins.org/
http://bit.ly/earnbtc (**survey**) http://earnthebitcoin.com/
http://bit.ly/lfnu1 (url shorten)
http://l.f.nu/?partner=15tZJ7sWuDJHgtYbyiymo1zbR3FkGkR
BTq
http://bit.ly/coinurl1 (url shorten) https://coinurl.com/
http://bit.ly/anonads (**ads**) http://anonymousads.com/
http://bit.ly/qmt5sL (**ads, and free btc**)
http://dailybitcoins.org/
http://bit.ly/coinad (**ads, and free btc**)
https://www.coinad.com/
http://bit.ly/5minbtc (**ads free btc**)
http://www.fiveminutecoin.com/
http://bit.ly/btckamikaze (**gamble**) http://bitcoin-
kamikaze.com/
http://bitcoin-kamikaze.com BitCoin LoTTo
http://bit.ly/btcminefield (**gamble**)
http://minefield.bitcoinlab.org/
http://bit.ly/bitcoindarts (**gamble**)
http://bitcoindarts.movoda.net
http://bit.ly/btcchess (**gamble**) Chess
www.fantasypublishings.com/
BitCoin Ptramid Features
http://bit.ly/bpyramid (**ads and pyramid scheme**)
http://bitcoinpyramid.com/
http://bit.ly/bidbtc (**pyramid**) http://bidonbitcoins.com/
http://bit.ly/btcmatrix (**pyramid**) http://btcmatrix.com/
http://bit.ly/sldoubler (**ponzi**) http://sldoubler.com/

http://bit.ly/smsdragon (**txt**) https://www.smsdragon.com/
http://bit.ly/btccalipers (**calipers**)
http://www.goldenmeancalipers.com/
http://bit.ly/btctrading (**forum**) http://www.bitcointrading.com/
Use BitCoins to buy domain and hosting services
http://bit.ly/bitdomain (**web host**) http://www.bitdomain.biz/
http://bit.ly/cinfu (**web host**) https://panel.cinfu.com/
http://bit.ly/btchost (**web hosting**)
http://www.btcwebhost.com/
http://bit.ly/joinorangewebsite (**web host**)
http://www.orangewebsite.com/affiliate/
http://bit.ly/surf4btc (**paid 2 surf**) http://surfformoney.net/ref/
http://pyramining.com/referral/

Underground Economy – basics

Reloadable Debit Cards

Basics

Greendot and other Reloadable debit cards can be used in an attempt to allow for anonymous financial transfer between customers and vendors. Vendors need to cash money out. They can accomplish this by setting up Greendot cards with stolen identities and getting them shipped to mail boxes set up with fake identification cards.

Customers need to load money in!

They can do this by going to any store that sells Greendot reload packs. Customers merely hand the clerk some cash and in return get a cardboard card with a load number on it. The customer can transfer this load number to the vendor via an encrypted and anonymous channel. The vendor then applies the loaded funds to the card via the internet. The loaded funds can then be cashed out at an ATM.

Security

These cards should be viewed as financial networks. The financial information consists of the traffic and the cards are the nodes. Reloadable debit card networks have a high degree of cross network contamination.

One additional network involved is the mail system, the vendor is required to have the card shipped to a physical mail box. This may not be particularly risky due to the fact that it is unlikely the card is being watched at this point as no customers are aware of it yet. However it is important for vendors to remember that the reloadable debit card company will keep their box information on record.

Another network the vendor needs to utilize is the telecommunications network. Vendors are required to talk over a telephone to activate the card. The risk inherent in this can be minimized if the vendor uses a burner phone. Vendors are also required to make an initial visit to a store in order to obtain their temporary card prior to being mailed one. CCTV cameras will likely record them. Customers also have to worry about CCTV cameras as they must hand money to a clerk in a store. Customers cannot take adequate measures to disguise their identity during this process as there is direct human interaction.

Reloadable debit cards have a distinct disadvantage of being highly centralized.

Vendors tend to have many customers send funding to a single centralized card. This means that a single compromised customer can compromise the Greendot card of the vendor. The only way to prevent this is for the seller to use multiple Greendot cards, one for each customer to be perfect. This is not very feasible.

If a malicious customer identifies the card of a vendor it is possible for network analysis to map out the financial network involved with this buyer. Records are kept of funds being transferred from a reload pack into cash out card. The time and location of reload pack sales that are used to fund cash out cards can be determined. A single compromised customer can use this information to gather video surveillance of every single person who has loaded funding to the card of the seller. This may not hold up as evidence by itself but it is strong intelligence indicating that a person who has sent funds to a vendor is in fact a drug customer.

Conclusion

Greendot and other Reloadable debit cards are not a safe means of conducting anonymous financial transfer. The financial networks created by these cards are very prone to network analysis. There is an unacceptable amount of cross network contamination for vendors. The load points for introducing finances into the network are also under too much surveillance.

Tips

Customers can outsource the purchase of reload moneyPaks. Good solutions may include utilizing bums and transients.

Vendors should avoid Greendot type reloadable debit cards. If they are used they should be highly compartmentalized (different cards for different groups of people).

Compartmentalization is not possible in all cases though. Remember, if a single customer is malicious they can compromise the entire compartment. This puts customers at risk as well!

Greendot cards are prone to being frozen. Triggers include typical patterns associated with narcotics trafficking; cashing out very soon after cashing in, getting payments from diverse geographic areas (geographic based compartmentalization of customers is suggested), particularly large amounts of money going through a card in a short period of time etc.

Western Union /Money Grams -Basics

Western Union and Moneygram money wires involve a customer sending funds to a vendor over the WU or MG financial network. Customers must go to a location that offers one of these services and hand money to a clerk. Depending on the country of the customer they may be required to show identification for any amount of money. In all locations identification must be shown for amounts of money over a certain limit, usually $500 or $1000. Customers fill out forms that are specially designed for gathering fingerprints and are usually under video surveillance.

Security

Despite their many shortcomings WU and MG both offer substantial benefits over reloadable debit cards. It is easier to use multiple pseudonyms for pick up from these services, the number of pseudonyms you have is limited only by the number of fake ID cards you can get. Unlike with Reloadable debit cards vendors are not required to use stolen identities. They are also not required to set up mailboxes or make telephone calls (WU). The ability to easily use multiple pseudonyms makes it easier to decentralize and compartmentalize the financial networks.

If a different fake ID is used for each customer, a single malicious customer will not be able to map out the entire network based on transaction records.

It is possible that a single malicious customer could use video surveillance and facial recognition to tie a multiple fake ID pseudonyms to a single person. After identifying the vendor in a single transaction facial recognition could identify them every time they send funding, even if they use a different fake identification document. This attack is possible but it is not likely to be used against drug traffickers at the current time.

One of the primary disadvantages of WU and MG is the fact that there are a limited number of locations a vendor can cash out from. Customers know the rough geographic area a vendor will pick up the wire from because when sending a WU or MG the city of the vendor must be listed on the form. This allows for surveillance teams to stake out a number of possible locations the pick up may be made at. These surveillance teams can be alerted when the target attempts pick up and then move in on the target. This risk is much smaller with Greendot cards because Greendot funding can be taken out from a large number of ATM's distributed through out a wide geographic area.

Tips

WU and MG have a substantial benefit over Greendot in that they can be used for funding E-currency. E-currency can dramatically increase the security of a financial transfer. Customers and vendors can and should use fake identification to counter the record keeping of transactions. Even if a vendor is legitimate customers may be flagged if they send large sums of money with their real identification. In some cases question and answer can be used to remove the need for identification. If this is allowed or not is highly dependent on the particular area of the customer/vendor Wearing gloves or avoiding finger contact with the forms can countermeasure-leaving fingerprints. Using stencils to fill out the forms at a private location can counter hand-writing analysis. However, video surveillance is something that cannot be countered.

Note: Forms are designed to pick up fingerprints

E-currency - Basics

Traditional E-currency systems (LR, PX) are relatively complex systems of financial transfer involving many companies. Usually an E-currency system is structured as follows:

a main digital gold company stores gold bars in a vault and creates audited cryptographically secure digital currency units. The main E-currency company runs a website that allows owners of the currency to manage their accounts as well as send and accept funding. Usually the main E-currency company is not interested in selling small amounts of currency. The main E-currency company will usually only sell large amounts of digital currency to exchanger companies. Average users of E-currency systems only deal with exchangers and use the main digital currency company only to manage their accounts.

E-currency exchangers are located around the world and they accept payment in various ways according to their own policy. Usually E-currency exchangers have no affiliation with the main E-currency company. Some exchangers are even scammers so be careful who you work with!

To load E-currency first you need to set up an account with the parent company. It is free to do this and usually requires no identification at best or at worst easy to forge identification. You should make sure to protect your anonymity when you set up E-currency accounts, at the very least you should use Tor or similar technology to protect from network forensics. Make sure the E-mail data you register with is no tied to you in anyway and was also obtained anonymously. After you have your account set up you will be given a number, which can be used to transfer currency to your account. Now you need to set up an order with an exchanger, it is suggested that you use offshore exchange services. How the exchanger accepts funding is totally up to their policy, many accept western union and some accept cash in the mail. After the exchanger gets the funding you send them they will transfer E-currency to your account minus a transaction fee. From here you can either send the E-currency to a vendors account or you can cash it out and have it sent to a vendor via another method through another exchanger. Exchanger's cash in and out meaning you cannot only buy E-currency from an exchanger for cash but you can also sell E-currency to an exchanger for cash.

Security
E-currency can be seen as similar to a financial multi-hop proxy, the first hop being the exchanger and the second hop being the E-currency company. This can add jurisdictional complication to financial network analysis attacks. You must make sure to follow normal operational security procedures when using E-currency, for example make sure to use anonymizer when interacting with the digital website and use fake identification for loading currency if possible. E-currency can also be used to create highly decentralized overlay networks, further adding to security of both customers and vendors.

Tips
If a vendor accepts WU but not E-currency customers can use E-currency to send WU. After loading E-currency merely cash it out via another exchanger to the WU details of the vendor.

Vendors can decentralize their financial networks by creating new E-currency accounts for each customer. Although this is time intensive the benefits are very extreme and it is highly suggested. If every customer is presented with a different E-currency account it will make it impossible for financial intelligence to map out customer networks. A malicious customer only knows the E-currency account they sent payment to, since no other customers sent payment to the same account the malicious customer gains no useful intelligence.

Vendors can appear to accept any payment method an exchanger offers while actually layering the funding through

E-currency accounts. When a customer places an order merely set up a request for funding with an E-currency exchanger and then present the customer with the funding information of the exchanger. The exchanger gets the funding from the customer and then puts it into the vendors E-currency account. This allows vendors to accept payment to any location they can find an exchanger in.

E-currency can be layered through multiple accounts prior to cashing out. It may be difficult for a legal team to prove an account that cashed out marked E-currency belongs to the same person who was sent the E-currency in the first place. Online E-currency casinos can be used to cheaply add more jurisdictions to a trace and potentially mix the finances of the vendor with many others. If a vendor loads E-currency to buy digital casino chips and then cashes the casino chips out for E-currency to a new account it will probably make it harder for financial intelligence agents to follow the trail and can unlink accounts from each other.

Trust Networks - Basics

Open trust networks are potentially a great way to cash out/in E-currency. Assume that Alice has obtained $10,000 worth of E-currency from her customers. Assume Alice and Bob are in a trusted relationship with each other. Perhaps Bob wants to purchase several thousand dollars worth of E-currency. Rather than go through an independent exchanger Bob may choose to send Alice his cash in return for E-currency. This allows Bob to obtain E-currency with high anonymity and also allows Alice to cash out via a trusted node. This can present a virtual dead end to financial intelligence teams. If the E-currency was watched they see it go to Bobs account but they do not know who Bob is or how he obtained the E-currency. Even if Bob paid for the E-currency via WU and was on CCTV, the agents will not know where the funding was sent. Cashing out of this system is eventually required unless the system continues to grow (Open versus Closed). Cashing out of a closed trust network can be done by Bob ordering product from another vendor and then selling it locally.

Borrowed Bank Accounts / Underground ATM cards

Borrowed bank accounts and underground ATM cards are useful for cashing out E-currency anonymously. They are also useful for taking bank wires as a method of payment. You need to be able to get the details of a bank account as well as a skim of the magnetic stripe of the ATM card tied to the account. If you can do this, you can cash the E-currency out through an exchanger via bank wire to the account you have a card for. You can now cash the money out at any ATM the card is accepted at. If you can get the skim of the ATM card, you can simply encode it to blank card stock for cashing out with.

I suggest not taking money out of the person's bank account unless you put it in. This will reduce the chances that they quickly notice you borrowed their bank account. You could leave extra money in the account as well, the person it belongs to may be less likely to report suspicious transactions if they are afraid they will lose whatever you left behind.

There are various organizations willing to offer ATM cards capable of being funded with E-currency and cashed out with at an ATM. Some of these services are scams and others are legit. Some require identification but these can be countered with fake documents.

Mule Networks

Mule networks can be used to help cash out funding. Obtaining a mule network is a difficult and time-consuming task. The most common technique is to offer 'work at home' job offers. People accept the job offer and are led to think that they are working for an official company when in reality they are merely picking up money and sending it on. It is expensive to fund these networks and only very realistic for large vendors. It is possible that feds will accept such offers in an attempt to perform human Sybil attacks on the networks formed.

Bitcoin

Bitcoin is a newer type of decentralized digital currency. The underlying system of Bitcoin is quite complex and difficult to summarize. It is suggested that you go to the BitCoin[1] website and learn about the system. There are various ways to anonymize Bitcoin transactions. As of 2011 June 14, bitCoins trade for approximately 20 US dollars per coin. A combination of Bitcoin and blind signature digital currency systems is likely the ideal way to cash in and out, however such systems are still largely experimental and developing. Additional laundry systems were available as a hidden services, however they have gone AWOL

FBI – BitCoin Report -Intelligence Assessment

Bitcoin Virtual Currency Report – Unclassified

(U) Bitcoin Virtual Currency: Unique Features Present
Distinct Challenges for Deterring Illicit Activity
24 April 2012
UNCLASSIFIED Intelligence Section
(U) A Bitcoin logo from https://en.bitcoin.it.

Executive Summary

(U//FOUO) Bitcoin – A decentralized,1 peer-to-peer (P2P)
network-based virtual currency –
provides a venue for individuals to generate, transfer,
launder, and steal illicit funds with some anonymity. Bitcoin
offers many of the same challenges associated with other
virtual currencies,
such as WebMoney, and adds unique complexities for
investigators because of it's decentralized
nature.
(U//FOUO) The FBI assesses with medium confidence2 that,
in the near term, cyber criminals
will treat Bitcoin as another payment option alongside more
traditional and established virtual
currencies, which they have little reason to abandon. This
assessment is based on fluctuations in
the Bitcoin exchange rate in 2011 and limited reporting
indicating bitCoins are being accepted as
payment by some cyber criminals.
(U//FOUO) The FBI assesses with low confidence, based on
current user and vendor acceptance,
Those malicious actors will exploit Bitcoin to launder money.
This assessment is based on
observed criminal activities, investigations, and prosecutions
of individuals exploiting other
virtual currencies, such as e-Gold and WebMoney. A lack of
current reporting specific to

Bitcoin restricts the confidence level.
(U//FOUO) Even though there is no central Bitcoin server to compromise, the FBI assesses with
high confidence, based on reliable industry and FBI reporting, that criminals intending to steal
bitCoins can target and exploit third-party BitCoin services and an individual's *Bitcoin wallet*.
Malicious actors can compromise personal computers and accounts using *malware* and hacking
techniques to steal users' bitCoins and use *botnets* to generate bitCoins.
(U//FOUO) Bitcoin will likely continue to attract cyber criminals who view it as a means to
move or steal funds as well as a means of making donations to illicit groups. If Bitcoin stabilizes
and grows in popularity, it will become an increasingly useful tool for various illegal activities
beyond the cyber realm. Since Bitcoin does not have a centralized authority, law enforcement
faces difficulties detecting suspicious activity, identifying users, and obtaining transaction
records – problems that might attract malicious actors to Bitcoin. Bitcoin might also logically
attract money launderers and other criminals who avoid traditional financial systems by using the
Internet to conduct global monetary transfers.
(U//FOUO) Although Bitcoin does not have a centralized authority, the FBI assesses with
medium confidence that law enforcement can identify, or discover more information about
malicious actors if the actors convert their bitCoins into a *fiat currency*. Third-party BitCoin
services may require customers to submit valid identification or bank information to complete
transactions. Furthermore, any third-party service that qualifies as a *money transmitter* must
register as a *money services business* with the Financial Crimes Enforcement Network (FinCEN)
and implement an anti-money laundering program.

1 (U) See Appendix A for a glossary of terms. All terms included in the glossary are italicized on their first use.
2 (U) See Appendix B for a description of confidence levels.

Scope Note

(U//FOUO) The Cyber and Criminal Intelligence Sections, with contributions from the FBI
Detroit Division, initiated this intelligence assessment to explore the unique aspects of the P2P
virtual currency Bitcoin. This assessment does not attempt to judge the likelihood of Bitcoins
long-term success as an alternate payment method, but explores how bitCoins (or any future
virtual currency similar to Bitcoin) are traded and how criminals can use them to conduct illicit
activity. This assessment draws primarily on intelligence from January 2011 through April 2012,
unless otherwise referenced for historical perspective.
(U//FOUO) This is the FBI's first Criminal and Cyber intelligence assessment related to Bitcoin.
In January 2012 the Counterterrorism Division disseminated an intelligence bulletin that
explored the potential to conduct illicit financial transactions using Bitcoin. Disseminated FBI
intelligence products on other virtual currencies include: (U) Cyber Criminal Exploitation of
Electronic Payment Systems and Virtual Currencies, dated 23 February 2011and (U) Cyber
Criminal Exploitation of Real-Money Trading, dated 8 June 2011, both of which discuss cyber
criminal misuse of virtual currencies for money laundering. While Bitcoin is a distinct virtual
currency, the overarching analytic judgments in this intelligence assessment about the use of
virtual currencies by criminal entities are consistent with these previous intelligence products.
(U//FOUO) This assessment will not address malicious actors outside of the cyber underground,

such as traditional organized crime groups, extremist groups, or child predators. Throughout the
paper, the term "Bitcoin," when capitalized, refers to both the open source software used to
create the virtual currency and the P2P network formed as a result; "BitCoin" using lower case
refers to the virtual currency that is digitally traded between users.

Source Summary Statement

(U//FOUO) The FBI used open source reporting extensively in this intelligence assessment, both in support of FBI reporting and to provide background information on Bitcoin. FBI sources vary from uncorroborated to highly reliable. FBI case information citing criminal activity is considered highly reliable because it is from FBI employees or FBI sources with direct access to the information.

(U//FOUO) Open source information comes from different online resources describing products or services offered to conduct monetary transactions and are, therefore, considered reliable.

(U//FOUO) The FBI acknowledges that participants in the BitCoin economy have an incentive to emphasize the popularity of Bitcoin. However, Bitcoin users also need reliable information about Bitcoin and the BitCoin exchange rate. For the purposes of this assessment, the FBI assumes that the body of open source information describing Bitcoin is generally indicative of the true state of the Bitcoin economy.

(U//FOUO) No contradictory information was found between FBI and open source reporting. Overall, the FBI considers the body of reporting to be consistent and plausible in the context of the BitCoin environment.

The Bitcoin Economy

· (U) As of 18 April 2012, the third-party BitCoin trading platform Mt. Gox recorded more than $8 million in transactions conducted over the past 30 days through Mt.Gox trading, an average of more than$276,000 per day.1

· (U) According to Bitcoin as of April 2012, there were more than 8.8 million bitCoins in circulation.2 With the average market price in April 2012 between $4 and $5 per BitCoin, the FBI estimates the Bitcoin economy was worth$35 million to $44 million.3,4

· (U) From May 2011 Bitcoin values fluctuated with exchange rates on Mt.Gox ranging as high as $30 in June 2011 to a low as $4 in December 2011.5

(U) Introduction

(U) Bitcoin3 is a decentralized, P2P network-based virtual currency that is traded online and exchanged into US dollars or other currencies. Bitcoin, when paired with third-party services, allows users to mine, buy, sell, or accept bitCoins from anywhere in the world. Bitcoins decentralized feature is unique among virtual currencies. While Bitcoin developers4,6maintain Web sites providing guidance to the Bitcoin community, they do not have a centralized database or authority. The P2Pnetwork issues bitCoins through the *mining* process and validates all transactions. Since Bitcoin does not have a centralized authority, detecting suspicious activity, identifying users, and obtaining transaction records is problematic for law enforcement.

(U) Despite the virtual nature of Bitcoin, users value the currency for many of the same reasons people trust Federal Reserve notes they believe they can exchange the currency for goods, services, or a national currency at a later date. As such, Bitcoin is currently accepted as a form of payment at hundreds of legitimate retailers including vendors selling clothing, games, music, and some hotels and restaurants.7

In addition, the unregulated nature of Bitcoin, combined with its other unique features, attracts criminals to this form of payment and transfer method.

Unique Features Present Distinct Challenges for Detecting and Stopping Illicit Activity

(U//FOUO) FBI reporting and analysis reveals that cyber criminals use electronic payment systems and virtual currencies5 as a way to launder money and to purchase or sell cyber goods and services in furtherance of their criminal objectives.8 Bitcoin, like these other virtual currencies, provides opportunities for criminals to transfer, launder, or steal funds. Bitcoin is unique because it is the only decentralized, P2P network-based virtual currency. The way it creates, operates, and distributes bitCoins makes it distinctively susceptible to illicit money transfers, and manipulation through the use of malware and botnets.

3 (U) See Appendix C for a description of how Bitcoin works.

4 (U) The Bitcoin source code is hosted on Github (https://github.com/bitcoin/bitcoin), a code sharing Web site where developers can work and submit changes. According to bitcoin.org there is a group of six core developers. These developers presumably control which changes are accepted on Github.

5 (U) For example, WebMoney, Liberty Reserve and Pecunix.(U//FOUO) All Bitcoin transactions are published online,9 but the only information that identifies a Bitcoin user is a pseudorandomly6 generated Bitcoin address, making the transactions somewhat anonymous (see text box). This potential anonymity is distinct from the anonymity provided by other electronic payment systems. For example, WebMoney and Liberty Reserve – which may allow users to register with false information, let suspicious activity go un noticed, or are located in a country that is not friendly to US law enforcement – still operate as companies with

centralized organization capable of instituting programs to ensure compliance with the Bank Secrecy Act (BSA).

(U///FOUO) As a decentralized digital currency system, Bitcoin lacks a centralized entity10 and is incapable of conducting due diligence (e.g., regulatory guidelines), monitoring and reporting suspicious activity, running an anti-money laundering compliance program, or accepting and processing legal requests like subpoenas.

(U) Bitcoins Used to Purchase Illicit Goods(U///FOUO) The FBI assesses with medium confidence that, in the near term, cyber criminals will treat Bitcoin as another payment option alongside more traditional and established virtual currencies such as WebMoney, which they have little reason to abandon. This assessment is6 (U) Bitcoin addresses are pseudorandom – defined by freedictionary.com as "of, relating to, or being random numbers generated by a definite, nonrandom computational process".

How Anonymous is Bitcoin?

(U) Bitcoins anonymity depends on the actions of the user. While some news articles have lauded Bitcoin as "untraceable digital currency,"11 the "About Bitcoin" page on bitcoin.org does not list anonymity as a feature of thecurrency.12 All Bitcoin transactions are published online and Internet Protocol (IP) addresses are linked to the public Bitcoin transactions. If a user does not anonymize his or her IP address, an interested party can identify the individual's physical location.13,14 Additionally, in July 2011 researchers from the University College Dublin, Ireland, demonstrated "the inherent limits of anonymity when using Bitcoin" by conducting passive analysis ofvarious types of public Bitcoin information, such as transaction records and user postings of public-private keys. The researchers suggest that law enforcement agencies or other centralized services (such as exchangers or retailers)
who have access to less public information (bank account information or shipping addresses) can connect even more

real world identifiers to Bitcoin wallets and transaction histories.15

What Users Can Do To Increase Anonymity
· (U)Create and use a new Bitcoin address for each incoming payment.
· (U) Route all Bitcoin traffic through an anonymizer.
· (U) Combine the balance of old Bitcoin addresses into a new address to make new payments.
· (U) Use a specialized money laundering service.
· (U) Use a third-party eWallet service to consolidate addresses. Some third-party services offer the option of creating an e-Wallet that allows users to consolidate many BitCoin address and store and easily access their bitCoins from any device.
· (U) Individuals can create Bitcoin clients to seamlessly increase anonymity (such as allowing user to choose which Bitcoin addresses to make payments from), making it easier for non-technically savvy users to anonymize their Bitcoin transactions.

Decentralized Authority Vulnerabilities
(U) No anti-money laundering software or monitoring capabilities to identify suspicious monetary patterns.
· (U) No identification of account owners or their actual location.
· (U) No historical records of transactions associated with real world identity.
· (U) More difficult to identify the original source of funds compared to other on line currencies.
· (U) Law enforcement cannot target one central location or company for investigative
purposes or to shut down the system. based on fluctuations in the BitCoin exchange rate in 2011 and limited reporting indicating bitCoins are being accepted as payment by some cyber criminals. If the exchange rate for bitCoins stabilizes and Bitcoin becomes more widely accepted by vendors and illicit sellers on the Internet, cyber criminals may increasingly

use bitCoins to purchase illegal goods and services and to fund illegal activities.

· (U///FOUO) As of October 2011, a cyber criminal selling a ZeuS botnet Trojan advised that he only accepted payments through Bitcoin, Liberty Reserve, or WebMoney, according to a collaborative source with good access, whose information has not been corroborated.

· (U) According to open source reporting as of June 2011, an online marketplace called Silk Road was selling illegal drugs and only accepted payment through Bitcoin. Silk Road allowed parties to communicate anonymously for the purchase and sale of illegal goods, to include the purchase of illegal narcotics, in addition to using Bitcoin. Customers could also leave feedback about their purchase experience in a system similar to other online sellers.
(U///FOUO) As of June 2011, a member of the online *Hacktivist* group LulzSec was using Bitcoin to purchase a botnet, according to an FBI source, some of whose reporting had been corroborated but that had been reported for less than one year.
(U///FOUO) According to open source reporting, as of June 2011 a member of LulzSec claimed the group had received over $18,000 in Bitcoins from fans and supporters.23

Bitcoin allowed LulzSec to receive donations without revealing the identities of the owners or the recipients. LulzSec provided updates about the donations they received by thanking donors publicly via status updates on the social networking site Twitter.

(U) Money Laundering
(U///FOUO) The FBI assesses with low confidence that malicious actors will exploit Bitcoin to launder money. The confidence level is based on observed criminal activities, investigations, and prosecutions of individuals laundering

money through other virtual currencies, such as e-Gold and WebMoney. Alack of reporting specific to Bitcoin restricts7 (U) In 2011 the exchange rate for bitCoins fluctuated from about $1/bitcoin in February to $30/bitcoin on 8 June to about $5/bitcoin in October. (www.bitcoincharts.com)the confidence level. Since Bitcoin does not have a centralized authority (see text box on page six), law enforcement faces difficulties in detecting suspicious activity, identifying users, and obtaining transaction records – problems that might attract malicious actors to Bitcoin. If Bitcoin becomes more widely accepted among vendors and users, the FBI anticipates seeing increased Bitcoin money laundering activities.

(U//FOUO) As of June 2011, organized criminal groups were using an online role playing game to facilitate money laundering by purchasing virtual game currency with the proceeds of criminal activity, according to an FBI sub-source of unknown reliability whose reporting has not been corroborated. The virtual game currency was used to purchase in-game virtual items that were then sold to other players for "clean money."

(U//FOUO) In August 2010 an FBI source with direct access but of undetermined reliability stated that he used fake names to register for WebMoney, a virtual currency electronic payment system, accounts which he used as part of a money laundering service. The source catered to cyber criminals who earned money from *carding* activities but who were not able to transfer money out of the United States by themselves.

(U//FOUO) The FBI further assesses with medium confidence, based on previously witnessed misuse of other virtual currencies, that malicious actors could increase their anonymity by laundering their bitCoins through third-party Bitcoin services registered outside the US. Some of these services act as exchangers or transmitters (see text box on page eight) that convert virtual currencies to fiat currencies (or other virtual currencies) or transfer bitCoins between members. Offshore services may provide additional anonymity by allowing currency exchange or money transfer without verifying user identification or enforcing any monetary exchange limits.

· (U//FOUO) As of June 2010 unknown subjects created 3,000 online membership accounts using 16,000 bank accounts at a US banking institution, according to a source with direct access and whose information has been corroborated. Using the online accounts, the perpetrators obtained fraudulent funds from victims by receiving payments for nonexistent auction items; these funds were then used to purchase gold from gold farmers. The subjects then sold this gold for *real money* – to others not linked to the malicious actors – using a dedicated third-party service.

· (U//FOUO) As of February 2009, an identified individual operated a Web site offering
money laundering services where cyber criminals could view the progress of there
transactions, according to a reliable, collaborative source with excellent access. The
individual laundered money using WebMoney.27

Theft of Bitcoins
(U//FOUO) The FBI assesses with high confidence, based on reliable industry and FBI reporting,
that criminals intending to steal bitCoins can target and exploit third-party Bitcoin services and an
individual's Bitcoin wallet, principally because there is no central Bitcoin server to compromise.
Malicious actors can compromise personal computers and accounts using malware and hacking
techniques to steal users' bitCoins. Additional techniques involve the creation of botnets to
compromise victim computers and servers instructing them to mine bitCoins.

· (U) In mid-June 2011 researchers from a major computer security firm, whose reporting
has been reliable in the past, discovered the malware "Infostealer.Coinbit" – the first
malware designed to steal bitCoins from compromised users' Bitcoin wallet. The malware
is capable of infecting users' computers and transferring their digital Bitcoin wallet to a
server in Poland.

· (U) In June 2011 a Bitcoin user posted a message on a Bitcoin forum stating that 25,000
of there bitCoins has been stolen from an unencrypted Bitcoin wallet on there
computer.37, 38, 39 At the June exchange rate of about $20 per BitCoin, the estimated value
of the loss was $500,000.

Third-Party Bitcoin Services
(U) Bitcoin, like most virtual currencies, requires individuals to use a third-party service to trade bitCoins for fiat currency. Buying, selling, or trading in bitCoins – or converting bitCoins into another currency – must be done using third-party businesses outside the Bitcoin P2P system. The number and diversity of these third-party businesses provide users with options for moving and potentially laundering their money.

(U) Various third-party BitCoin services can, or are used to, facilitate trade between individuals and businesses, buy and sell bitCoins, or convert bitCoins into other currencies.31 Users who do not want to use an intermediary third-party can also post "buy" and "sell" orders on #bitcoin-otc, a Bitcoin marketplace located on the *freenode Internet relay chat* (IRC) network.

(U) In July 2011 FinCEN revised the definition of "money transmission service" to mean "the acceptance of currency, funds, or other value that substitutes for currency from one person and the transmission of currency, funds or other

value to another location or person by any means." It is likely that the business models of many third-party BitCoin services qualify them as money transmitters, and therefore money services businesses (MSB),under 31 CR Part 1010.100(ff)(5). Third-party BitCoin services that qualify as money transmitters and who wish to operate legitimately must register with FinCEN, implement anti-money laundering programs, retain certain records, and file suspicious activity reports and currency transactions reports as required. Additionally, since any third-party Bitcoin service that falls under the MSB rule would do so as a money transmitter, there is not a transaction threshold (such as 1,000 per day) that must be met for the regulations to apply, unlike dealers in
foreign exchange or issuers or sellers of checks or monetary instruments.34 (Note: In certain states, third-party BitCoin services would also be required to obtain a state license).

(U//FOUO) Law enforcement might have opportunities to discover real user identifying information from some third-party Bitcoin services because users must provide the services with real payment account information to buy, sell, trade, and convert their bitCoins. For example, the Terms of Service for the third-party BitCoin trading platform Mt. Gox states "members agree to provide Mt. Gox with accurate, current and complete information about themselves as promoted by the registration process, and keep such information updated."35

(U) On 19 June 2011, a compromise involving the third-party BitCoin trading platform Mt. Gox led to an attempt to sell $7 million in bitCoins, driving the trading price to near zero before trading was suspended.

· (U//FOUO) According to a complaint received by the FBI's Internet Crime Complaint Center in April 2011, an individual had 680 bitCoins stolen from his online game site. At the time of this incident the market price was $8 per BitCoin, creating a loss of $5,440.43

Theft of Services for the Purpose of Mining Bitcoins
(U//FOUO) FBI and open source reporting indicates that malicious actors can exploit the way bitCoins are generated by compromising victim computers and instructing them to mine bitCoins. Criminals first install malware on a victim's computer, then use these compromised computers to generate bitCoins.

(U/FOUO) An identified Internet security researcher who has reported reliability in the past identified ZeuS malware that installed software that mined bitCoins. This ZeuS software was spread by links placed on an identified social networking site.

(U) According to unconfirmed open source reporting from a major periodical whose reporting has proven reliable in the past, a botnet made up of 100,000 infected computers could be used to generate $7,500 worth of bitCoins per day, at late June 2011 exchange rates, by using the computing resources of victim machines.

(U) Since large-scale BitCoin mining requires a large amount of costly processing power and electrical energy, some miners have resorted to "borrowing" processing power from large computing clusters through computer intrusion. In addition to unauthorized access to networks, there have been incidents where unauthorized use of a network had been linked to Bitcoin mining.

· (U//FOUO) FBI reporting from a reliable source indicated that in late May 2011, an unknown actor used several machines on a computing cluster at an identified Mid western university to manufacture bitcoins.46 As of 26 May 2011, two IP addresses were used to compromise 22 machines and six computer clusters. On 29 May 2011, two different IP addresses compromised an additional five workstations and two computer clusters. The unknown actor then used the compromised computers to access networks at three other identified universities and tried to gain access to two government facilities.

(U//FOUO) According to unconfirmed open source reporting, a system administrator for a college near New York City admitted in a May 2011 interview to using the school's computers for Bitcoin mining unbeknownst to the school.

Bitcoins Outlook and Implications
(U//FOUO) Bitcoin will likely continue to attract cyber criminals who view it as a means to transfer, launder, or steal funds as well as a means of making donations to groups participating in illegal activities, such as Hacktivist. As long as there is a means of converting bitCoins into real money, criminal actors will have an incentive to steal them. Since maintaining anonymity while using Bitcoin requires that users not exchange or transfer their bitCoins using third-party bitCoins services that require real world account information, the use of bitCoins to make donations to dis reputable groups (which can be done within the Bitcoin P2P system) will likely remain one of the most popular uses for the virtual currency.

(U//FOUO) If Bitcoin stabilizes and grows in popularity, it will become an increasingly useful
tool for various illegal activities beyond the cyber realm. For instance, child pornography and
Internet gambling are illegal activities already taking place on the Internet which require simple
payment transfers. Bitcoin might logically attract money launderers, human traffickers, terrorists,
and other criminals who avoid traditional financial systems by using the Internet to conduct
global monetary transfers.

(U//FOUO) Although Bitcoin does not have a centralized authority, the FBI assesses with
medium confidence that law enforcement can discover more information about, and in some

cases identify, malicious actors, if the actors convert their bitCoins into a fiat currency. Third party BitCoin services may require customers to submit valid identification or bank information to complete transactions. Furthermore, any third-party service that qualifies as a money transmitter, and therefore a MSB, must register with the FinCEN and implement an anti-money laundering program.

Bitcoins Intelligence Gaps
· (U//FOUO) Who is using Bitcoin to circumvent BSA regulations (e.g., money launderers)?
· (U//FOUO) Which third-party Bitcoin services support illegal activity?
· (U//FOUO) Which criminal, nation state, and terrorist organizations are using Bitcoin to finance their operations?

(U) Intelligence Collection Requirements Addressed in Paper
(U//FOUO) This intelligence assessment will address requirements contained in the following FBI National Standing Collection Requirements topics: Botnets contained in WW-BOT-CYDSR-0027-11, Money Laundering contained in USA-MLA-CID-0032-10, Cyber Intrusions with a Criminal Nexus contained in WW-CYBR-CYD-SR-0061-10, and Virtual Worlds/Online Games contained in WW-CYBER-CYD-SR-0028-11.

(U) This assessment was prepared by the Domestic Threats Cyber Intelligence Unit, Technology Cyber Intelligence Unit, and the Financial Crimes Intelligence Unit of the FBI. Comments and queries may be addressed to the unit chiefs at 202-651-3051, 202-651-3139 or 202-324-8629, respectively.

Appendix A: FBI report Key Terms

(U) Bitcoin wallet: A data file that stores BitCoin currency (see appendix C). A user downloads
software to a personal computer or may use an online, third-party provider to create a wallet
(often called an eWallet) to store bitCoins.

(U) Botnets: Any group of two or more computers and/or mobile devices that are controlled
and/or updated remotely for an illegal purpose. Botnets can be used to perform denial of service
attacks, send spam e-mail, host illegal content, and may aid in most other types of online
criminal behavior.

(U) Carding: the act of trafficking and/or fraudulent use of stolen credit card account
information.

(U) Decentralized: No central administration, issuing authority, or database.

(U/FOUO) Cyber underground: The extensive network of members engaged in cyber crime
activities that have a unique language, an underground economy, a set of expectations about its
members' conduct, and a system of social stratification based on knowledge, skill, and activities.

(U) Electronic payment systems: Provide a secure means of transferring money among parties
to facilitate e-commerce and operate using real money or virtual currency. Electronic payment
systems either allow payment to be made between users, vendors, and other merchants, or they
only allow payments to be made between users or accounts. There is both a regulated sector and
a sector operating outside regulatory systems.

(U) Exchangers: Online entities that, for a fee, convert cash, virtual currency, or digital gold
currency into the type of currency requested. In general, individuals must use an exchanger to
deposit money into an electronic payment system account, unless the electronic payment system
has a physical location. Due to this fact, exchangers are a vital part of the money flow for
electronic payment systems and virtual currencies.

(U) Fiat Currency: Money that has value solely due to government regulation or law. Most
modern currencies, such as the US dollar and the Euro are fiat currencies.

(U) Freenode: An open source software-focused Internet relay chat network.

(U) Hacktivist: Individuals or groups who attack computer systems to draw attention to a
particular issue, influence public opinion, or punish perceived entities that oppose there
ideological positions.

(U) Internet Relay Chat (IRC): A form of real-time Internet synchronous conference, mainly
designed for group communication in discussion forums called channels, but also allowing one to-
one communication via private messages.

(U) Malware or malicious software: Computer software that facilitates illicit activities, too
include data ex-filtration, denial of service attacks, fraud, and spam dissemination.
(U) Mining, Bitcoin (also known as Bitcoin Creation, Bitcoin Generation, and Bitcoin
Manufacturing): The process of allowing the Bitcoin network to use a computer's resources in

exchange for the possibility of earning bitCoins. The more computing power a user offers, the
more likely they are to receive bitCoins.

(U) Money services business (MSB): Any person doing business in one or more of the following capacities, wholly or in substantial part within the United Sates: 1.) dealer in a foreign exchange; 2.) check casher; 3.) issuer or seller of traveler's checks or money orders; 4.) issuer, seller, or redeemer of stored value; 5.) money transmitter; 6.) U.S. Postal Service (31 C.F.R103.11).

(U) Money transmitter: A person that provides money transmission services. The term "money
transmission services" means the acceptance of currency, funds, or other value that substitutes
for currency from one person and the transmission of currency, fund, or other value that
substitutes for currency to another location or person by any means.

(U) Peer-to-Peer (P2P): A type of network in which each workstation has equivalent
capabilities and responsibilities. P2P is typically used for the transfer of data from one peer to
another and are free programs that can be easily downloaded from the Internet. P2P file-sharing
is the primary source for pirated software. Some popular examples include Limewire, Kazaa, and
Gnutella.

(U) Public Key Cryptography (PKI): A framework for creating a secure method for exchanging information based on public key cryptography. PKI uses a certificate authority (CA),which issues digital certificates that authenticate the identity of organizations and individuals over a public system such as the Internet.

(U) Real money: Coins or paper notes issues and backed by a government and used as a medium of exchange and measure of value.

(U) Virtual currency: Something used on the Internet that is in circulation as a medium of exchange but is not backed by a government.

(U) ZeuS Trojan: malicious software used by cyber criminals to steal online account credentials.

Appendix B: Confidence Levels
(U) High confidence generally indicates that FBI judgments are based on high-quality information from multiple sources or a single highly reliable source, or that the nature of the issue makes it possible to render a solid judgment.

(U) Medium confidence generally means that the information is interpreted in various ways, that the FBI has alternating views, or that the information, while credible, is of insufficient reliability to warrant a higher level of confidence.

(U) Low confidence generally means that the information is scant, questionable, or very fragmented; that it is difficult to make solid analytic inferences; or that the FBI has significant concerns or problems with the source.
(
U) Appendix C: *How Does Bitcoin Work?*
(U) To use Bitcoin, an individual first downloads and installs the free Bitcoin software (client). The application uses *Public Key Cryptography* (PKI) to automatically generate a Bitcoin address where the user can receive payments. The address is a unique 36 character-long string of numbers and letters and is stored in a user's virtual "wallet" on his or her local file system. Users can create as many Bitcoin addresses as they like to receive payments and can use a new address for every transaction they receive.

(U) To send bitCoins, users input the address they would like to send their bitCoins to and the amount of bitCoins they would like to transfer. The user's computer then digitally signs the transaction and sends the information to the distributed, P2P Bitcoin network. The P2P network verifies that the person sending the bitCoins is the current owner of the bitCoins they are sending, prohibiting a malicious user from spending the same bitCoins twice. Once the transaction has been validated by the Bitcoin network, receivers can spend the bitCoins they have received. This process usually takes a few minutes and is not reversible.

(U) The Bitcoin software program controls the rate of BitCoin creation, but it does not control the market value of a BitCoin; the market value is determined by the supply of bitCoins in circulation and people's desire to hold or trade bitcoins.52, 53 Unlike most fiat currencies, in which central banks can arbitrarily increase the supply of currency, Bitcoin is designed to eventually contain21 million bitCoins; no additional coins will be created after that point, preventing inflation.

(U) Bitcoin was created in such a way that the clients "mine" bitCoins at a predetermined rate. This chart illustrates the growth rate from 2009 to 2033, the year the last new BitCoin will be created.
Source: (U) Internet site; Bitcoin Wiki; "Controlled Currency Supply"; https://en.bitcoin.it/wiki/Controlled_Inflation; accessed in 5 March 2012; The source is a community wiki aimed at allowing anyone to freely document information about Bitcoin. Users must create a free account with a valid e-mail address to edit the Bitcoin Wiki.

Bitcoin Mining Scam
We found -this in the (.onion network site) Black-Market Reload (while looking into BitCoin mining. BitCoin mining is something that people are getting into and using customize

scripts to use zombie computers to generate bitCoins. Using Trojan-Downloader.win32.Agent.bmzd as a starting point it is modified to give its own unique hash file that will sometimes be overlooked by virus scans.

Then the author will insert 2 miners for him and give you the rest. At least that's what this ad tells us. Here is a clue what a scan is it says it does not draw CPU power and of course if you know anything about Mining bitCoins that's how it hashes bitCoins. So I would think that it would slow down a windows machine quite a bit. Since it modeled as a legit BitCoin Miner they tell us it's 100% undetectable, I question that part. I also see that they are using DeepBit guild instead of the BTC guild, BTC guild will give you a little higher hashes and faster.

GREED is the reason why this little scam will work. The old saying if it's too good to be true it's NOT true. As bitCoins become more popular we will see others come into the BitCoin mining, but think about it. You can now take over a machine and have it mine BitCoins. It's pretty much undetectable because the zombie machine is not being use to DDOS someone or used as a spammer machine. These zombies will be noticed when the C2 (Control and Control) is

caught but in this BitCoin scam the machines will not be

Figure 46 - BitCoin

noticed too much from the outside world just the user will have a slow ass Windows machine- let's face it a slow Windows machine is normal, and since this is only marketed in the DeepWeb not the clearWeb less people will notice the Ad can be found in the deepWeb-

http://4eiruntyxxbgfv7o.onion/paste/show.php?id=169a82809 0203b12

Figure 47 - Stealth BitCoin Miner

Hi! I'm android2 and in this site http://5onwnspjvuk7cwvk.onion/index.php?p=view_listing&id =2851
(The WELL known Black-Market Reloaded) I sell this really.. REALLY cheap.
(you must sing up to enter… just do it as customer, enter nickname..
and you're IN! .. then enter http://5onwnspjvuk7cwvk.onion/index.php?p=view_listing&id =2851)
As you'll see.. I have positive feedback.. I'm not a scamming newbie.. I just want to spread and
get people to know what I sell!
What is it? {It's EXTREMELY well described in the item description}

.. I will paste the item description below ;).. please at least visit it!
100% Coded By Myself, Undetectable, Customized… and STEALTH!
****

Proof it is "undetectable":
https://www.virustotal.com/file/ef390fc5455a3a2ca07168eff0 5071d10bf7ed156d2455fb28e5b6eb045ddb7f/analysis/1335 995324/
.. notice that the ONLY positive was from Byte Hero ONLY.. and it is even a FALSE positive.. "Trojan-Downloader.win32.Agent.bmzd" because it doesn't download anything. It passed ALL Antivirus.
****

How does it work? Well…
I make a CUSTOMIZED and UNIQUE Stealth miner exe (configured with 2 worker sessions of yours), I send it to you, and you and make your victims execute it (I can disguise it as you wish just ASK… **for example I spread mine in a forum**. I embedded a legitimate Windows7 activator.. and while actually activating Windows7.. it , **without popup of ANY kind, it generated some files.. and starts mining**)
It draws a little of GPU Power form each machine, mining for you! I've spread mine, and in one month now I have already Passed the 2000Mhash/s!
Excellent for posting anywhere… just make me disguise the exe! , **uploading to your BOT-NET**, or **infect with social engineering**, or, if you want to, embed a useful EXE, disguise it, and while actually executing the legitimate EXE… also **installing the Silent Miner**.
It's 100% made by me. It hides itself. Auto-start with windows… NO window opened. **Doesn't draw CPU power!**
The victim will not notice! No strange windows, no console popup… NOTHING!
The best part: 100% Undetectable! It's based on a nodded and legitimate GPU Miner, so it can't be detected as VIRUS!

IT DOESN'T AUTO SPREAD ITSELF… so the key is how many victims execute this… thinking a bit you'll came with TONS of ways (ask me to change the icon, a fake screen error, embedding a legitimate binary..) Thanks to that, get almost 100% invisibility to Heuristics.

Once executed by the victim.. the victim can even delete the original file.. because the files are already installed!

It's simple. All you need to give me is the data of 2 workers (recommend BIG Public Mining Pools.. for anonymity.. and quick cash out.. I used **Deepbit** for example) (One is backup in case the first one's mining pool is down). That is Miner address and password {the password of the miner, not session… ask if you don't understand this.. it's not dangerous, because it's the pass of the worker}. And the things you want me to do … put a custom icon? embedding a some sort of file or binary? ASK for it!

IMPORTANT: Once made the program and shipped to you, the workers address can't be changed by ANY MEANS, because it's embedded to the code.

I sold the first for 0.35 now it is a bit higher … Check the feedback yourself! it works! Have your Own Miner Factory… without having to spend money on hardware. With this, is extremely EASY to make much more in a day, than the price I ask for it. You'll get that money back in NO TIME.

The price is extremely low to the Next buyers just to get positive feedback of the product.. I'm planning to sell it for more than 2BTC or something like that. (In matter of days I got 2BTC from mine…)

. Consider this discount as a EXTREMELY good opportunity to get a 100% anonymous, decentralized, and secure way to get BTC!

CUSTOM THINGS I MAY ADD IF YOU ASK FOR (Check "Shipping options", some of these are free, others not… if you only want the free ones, select the option one, to complete the price of the offer :)):

*Error Message – FREE {Once the victim machine executes it, you can chose it to do nothing -silent, no popup, no window, nothing-, or if you want it to be used with Social Engineering, show some sort of error message}

*Exec's Icon – FREE {Change the icon of the file… useful for social engineering
*Embed File/Binary – 0.09BTC Extra {You can ask me to embed -you must provide it- a file, so the victim won't suspect it's something weird happening. For example, I embedded a USEFUL Windows 7 Activator, and made the spread SO easy… because it actually unlocked Windows7 while infecting with the miner, so they shared it to friends and leave positive feedback on the post}
*YOU can say whatever you need and I will try to adapt this to your needs!
I'm doing it with LOW price because I want positive feedback to this product in particular {because it's made by myself}. Then I'll set a HIGHER Price.
If you have any doubts, please ASK… don't keep the doubts!
- BITCOIN Silent FUD GPU Miner,UNDETECTABLE,100%Custom.

How Normal Business can use ToR

Hide Scada In The Tor Network – ..-Hiding In Plain Site..

We can -now provide your company a FREE .onion network – reliable 24/7 secure / encrypted / untraceable communication between your SCADA systems talking to each other and the main office giving you real-time data from any remote SCADA site.
As an example from Scheider Electric white paper on – Video Surveillance Integrated with SCADA – White Paper – we can now take that physical video security of all your remote video assets and transmit them securely, encrypted and untraceable to anyplace in the world to your datacenter.

Figure 48 - SCADA Communication

When going in and out of the invisible .onion network, you

SCADA Communication Methods

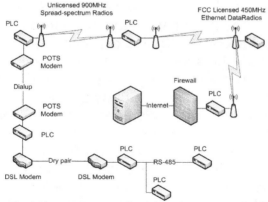

can control the entry and exit relays so picking safe verified relays to use is easy, or you can use your own relays, the more relays the better the system becomes at making you more invisible.

The more people that use it the more untraceable and unmonitored it becomes. This kind of SCADA communication in the ToR- onion network redefines geo-political digital boundaries. Since it rides on any Internet connection it can be used anywhere. In the ToR-.onion network merchants can't spy on you and they can't steal your information *Not if but when* —business take over the ToR- .onion network it will change the landscape and give it more order but it will still give the user anonymity that's the key to this network your signal, your voice cannot be found but you can still communicate. The ToR- .onion network rides not on top or the bottom of the digital super-highway but thru it.

Let's keep in mind that access to the ToR-.onion network is FREE to anyone and your company's use of the network makes it safer for everyone since the more people use it the more unreachable-undetectable you become.

But in business you also have to deal with hostile governments and protecting your people and assets thru a ToR .onion network becomes even more critical. You can still operate but be safe and secure in your business communications.

The ToRProject.org is something that is making an impact on the very lives of people that want to have a free safe secure voice. Just look at Mr. Chen a dissident from China he was jailed because he spoke up about the disable in China. The ToRProject.com helps people like Mr. Chen speak and to remain in anonymity. But by adding real business -relays into the ToR- .onion network we will give these people and the business more transparency, it makes you more invisible on the internet. You can donate to the ToR project and it's a 501(c), so it's deductible. Look at the donors list and see who support this invisible network. U.S Naval Research, National Science Foundation- DARPA – National Christian Foundation are some of the people supporting the ToR Project, it's not so bad if they use it— see lab Notes below -

How you going to hack what you can't find, can't see and can't trace to you?

Just think **Mr. bankers a free secret untraceable encrypted-communication** place where you can **do your banking deals** -in secret- and nobody but you and your closes friends know it even exist, not the government, not your spouse and harder for criminals to find your valuable data. It hides you in an Internet bubble of packets were nobody knows who you are or how to find you. Try can't even tell it's a ToR- .onion network it hides its signal to blend into the bits and bytes of the landscape in the digital noise. Technically it **pretty cheap** get the **free software** as many copies as you need FREE!!! No volume-pricing no updates FREE!!! Once your computer that talks to the internet hooks up to a ToR- Relays it's in the matrix. If you add your own ToR-Relays you can use trusted Relays as entry and exit nodes into the ToR-.onion network so you can let the program use it randomness or choose a path into a FREE invisible comunication media accessible from any Internet connection. -
The ToRProject.org is currently still fighting censorship and monitoring in China, Iran, Syria and others were people are being killed and sent home in small boxes to their relatives. Because that person could not use a ToR-network access to his Gmail account that was monitored they showed him his emails and his guilt and killed him. That's how brutal it can become if you cannot have a safe secure access to a basic email to communicate with the world. Government will kill you for what you say. Donate to the ToRProject.org
It's easy -if all else fails call us we can help your business become invisible in/on the Internet.

We use the ToR network for all communication in SCADA systems. Here are a few SCADA White papers try them with ToR- .onion Networks.

Optimizing a Wireless Ethernet Radio Network – White Paper (http://www.controlmicrosystems.com/media/page-body-files/white-papers/SE-WhitePaper-8.5x11-OptimizingWirelessEthernet-V004.pdf)

Video Surveillance Integrated with SCADA – White Paper
(http://www.clearscada.com/media/downloads/white-papers/Video_Surveillance_Integrated_with_SCADA.pdf)

Modbus and DNP3: Comparing Communication Efficiencies – White Paper
(http://www.controlmicrosystems.com/media/page-body-files/white-papers/Modbus_vs_DNP3_whitepaper.pdf)

Antenna and Feedline Selection – White Paper
(http://www.controlmicrosystems.com/media/page-body-files/white-papers/Antenna%20and%20Feedline%20Selection%20-%20White%20Paper%20%28Rev%206%29.pdf)

ClearSCADA Enhanced Report Management Tools for Large and Small Utilities – White Paper
(http://www.controlmicrosystems.com/media/page-body-files/white-papers/WP_3.pdf)

ClearSCADA Integrated Developer Environment (IDE) – White Paper
(http://www.controlmicrosystems.com/media/page-body-files/white-papers/WP_4.pdf)

ClearSCADA Redundancy – White Paper
(http://www.controlmicrosystems.com/media/page-body-files/white-papers/WP_5.pdf)

The Future is Here – White Paper
(http://www.controlmicrosystems.com/media/page-body-files/white-papers/WP_11.pdf)

Well Head Automation Made Simple – White Paper
(http://www.controlmicrosystems.com/media/page-body-files/white-papers/WP_11.pdf)

A Review of Wireless Networks – White Paper
(http://www.controlmicrosystems.com/media/page-body-files/white-papers/WP_1.pdf)

SCADA Systems – Looking Ahead – White Paper
(http://www.controlmicrosystems.com/media/page-body-files/white-papers/WP_10.pdf)

Effects of Atmospheric Pressure on Gas Measurement – White Paper
(http://www.controlmicrosystems.com/media/page-body-files/white-papers/WP_8.pdf)

Dual Redundant Controller Systems – White Paper
(http://www.controlmicrosystems.com/media/page-body-files/white-papers/Dual%20Redundant%20Controller%20Systems%20-%20White%20Paper.pdf)

The Top 6 Reasons to Upgrade to DNP3 Communications
(http://www.controlmicrosystems.com/media/page-body-files/white-papers/SE-WhitePaper-8.5x11-DNP3Communications-V002.pdf)

Coal Bed Methane Well Automation – White Paper
(http://www.controlmicrosystems.com/media/page-body-files/white-papers/WP_6.pdf)

Exchanging Data Between ClearSCADA and Other Applications – White Paper
(http://www.controlmicrosystems.com/media/page-body-files/white-papers/CS%20db%20xhange.pdf)

Tor: Sponsors
The Tor Project's diversity of users means we have a diversity of funding sources too — and we're eager to diversify even further! Our sponsorships are divided into levels based on total funding received:

- *Magnoliophyta* (over $1 million)
- An anonymous North American NGO (2008-2012)
- Broadcasting Board of Governors (2006-2011)
- *Liliopsida* (up to $750k)
- Sida – Swedish International Development Cooperation Agency (2010-2012)
- *Asparagales* (up to $500k)
- Internews Europe (2006-2008)
- National Science Foundation via Drexel University (2009-2011)
- *Alliaceae* (up to $200k)
- You or your organization?
- *Allium* (up to $100k)
- NLnet Foundation (2008-2009)
- Naval Research Laboratory (2006-2010)
- An anonymous North American ISP (2009-2012)
- *Allium cepa* (up to $50k)
- More than 2700 personal donations from individuals like you (2006-2012)
- Google (2008-2009)
- Google Summer of Code (2007-2011)
- Human Rights Watch (2007)
- Torfox (2009)
- Shinjiru Technology (2009-2011)
- National Christian Foundation (2010-2012)
- Past sponsors
- We greatly appreciate the support provided by our past sponsors in keeping the pre-501(c)(3) Tor Project progressing through our ambitious goals:
- Electronic Frontier Foundation (2004-2005)
- DARPA and ONR via Naval Research Laboratory (2001-2006)

- Cyber-TA project (2006-2008)
- Bell Security Solutions Inc (2006)
- Omidyar Network Enzyme Grant (2006)
- NSF via Rice University (2006-2007)

Wikipedia
http://en.wikipedia.org/wiki/SCADA
SCADA (supervisory control and data acquisition)
generally refers to industrial control systems (ICS): computer systems that monitor and control industrial, infrastructure, or facility-based processes, as described below:
Industrial processes include those of manufacturing, production, power generation, fabrication, and refining, and may run in continuous, batch, repetitive, or discrete modes.
Infrastructure processes may be public or private, and include water treatment and distribution, wastewater collection and treatment, oil and gas pipelines, electrical power transmission and distribution, wind farms, civil defense siren systems, and large communication systems.
Facility processes occur both in public facilities and private ones, including buildings, airports, ships, and space stations. They monitor and control HVAC, access, and energy consumption.
A SCADA system usually consists of the following subsystems:
A human–machine interface or HMI is the apparatus or device, which presents process data to a human operator, and through this, the human operator monitors and controls the process.
A supervisory (computer) system, gathering (acquiring) data on the process and sending commands (control) to the process.
Remote terminal units (RTUs) connecting to sensors in the process, converting sensor signals to digital data and sending digital data to the supervisory system.
Programmable logic controller (PLCs) used as field devices because they are more economical, versatile, flexible, and configurable than special-purpose RTUs.

Communication infrastructure connecting the supervisory
system to the remote terminal units.
Various process and analytical instrumentation

The Dark-net and Cyber Crime

Cyber Crime

Every day we exchange personal information with colleagues, friends and unknown people with no idea how they are treated and for what use they will be managed. Telephone number, email address or driver's license number are example of the data we provide ordinary using new media channels like internet and the social networks.
The use of this information is of great interest for the industry of crime because it is possible to commit a wide range frauds with high profits.
With the terms Identity Theft and identity fraud are referred all types of crime in which an ill-intentioned individual obtains and uses another person's personal data, this kind of crimes are increasing according the data provided by law enforcement all over the world.
Many organizations have tried to provide a characterization of the phenomenon trying to classify the types of identity theft in categories.
SANS Institute proposed the following characterization:

- Financial fraud – type of identity theft that includes bank fraud, credit card fraud, computer and telecommunications fraud, social program fraud, tax refund fraud, mail fraud, and many more. A total of 25 types of financial identity fraud are investigated by the United Secret Service.
- Criminal activities – type of identity fraud involves taking someone else's identity in order to commit a crime, enter a country, get special permits, hide one's own identity, or commit acts of terrorism. Criminal activities can include:
  - Computer and cyber crimes

- o Organized crime
- o Drug trafficking
- o Alien smuggling
- o Money laundering

How do identity thieves access personal information?
There are a lot of scenarios to access to personal information and identify them is necessary to recognize and prevent this type of crime. Most common case are:
- through a social engineering attack
- through a retail transaction
- by hacking into computer systems
- through phishing campaigns
- through stolen purses or wallets
- through stolen personal documents
- by stealing information from a company who had stored the data online
- through stolen mail
- and in many other ways
- through dumpster diving – rummaging through trash in an attempt to find personal information

How widespread is the crime and what are the figures that show its growth?

A global precise estimates of phenomenon is impossible due to the different legal treatment reserved for this type of crime in different countries, however, to provide a valid indication I extrapolated some data from the "2012 Identity Fraud Report 2011" study conducted by Javelin Strategy & Research.
The company collects data related to US citizens to measure the overall impact of identity fraud on consumers. In the next graphics is presented the progress of the Incident Rate from 2003.

The situation is worrying, 4.9% of U.S. Adults Were Victims of Fraud in 2011. After a sensible reduction of identity fraud incidence from 2009 to 2010, we see an increase this year of more than 10%. ID fraud increased to 4.90% in 2011 from 4.35% in 2010, which represents a 12.6% increase. The total number of identity fraud victims increased to about 11.6 million U.S. adults in 2011, compared to 10.2 million victims in 2010.

Despite the growth of incidents for ID fraud, the annual overall fraud amount was at its lowest point of $18 billion since 2003 attributable to the rapid increase of thefts characterized by lower profits.

4.9% of U.S. Adults Were Victims of Fraud in 2011

Figure 1: Fraud Incidence Rate, 2003-2011

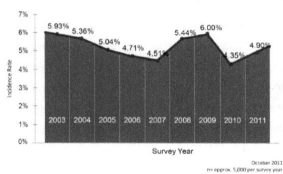

October 2011
n= approx. 5,000 per survey year
Base: All consumers.
© 2012 Javelin Strategy & Research

Digital Identity

Particularly alarming is the growth of such crimes in computers. Which are the information that compose our digital identity?

On the Internet, our identity composed by:

- IP (Internet Protocol) address
- address where we live
- usernames
- passwords
- personal identification numbers (PINs)

- social security numbers
- birth dates
- account numbers
- other personal information

The data are continuously exposed to high risk of frauds, the propensity of Internet users to the usage social networks and the rapid spread of mobile platforms create the right conditions for criminals.
Unlike the classic identity theft, for digital theft victims don't have to wait for a thief to physically steal their information that can be stolen by computer criminals from the databases of banks, retailers, ISPs and also from victim's PC.
In internet researches have identified three main schemas to realize identity thieves

- **Phishing Attacks** – This lure often comes in the form of a spam email or pop-up warning that looks like it has been sent from a company we trust. Often the companies are ones that we use regularly, like our bank, credit card company or some other online payment system. If we click on the link indicated, we are directed to a web site that is designed to look exactly like the official site of the company being miss-represented. Under the assumption that they are at an official site, victims enter specific personal information, such as social security number, credit card number or password.

- **Malware technology** – The fraud is realized when users download malware just by clicking on a pop-up ad or viewing spam email. The malware gathers information, such as user IDs and passwords for bank accounts, logging all keyboard strokes, or by using Trojans and other techniques to collect information from our PCs. This information is then passed back to the Command and Control servers when victims connect to the Internet.

- ***Pharming*** – In pharming, a cyber criminal exploits a vulnerability in an ISP's (Internet Service Provider) DNS server and hijacks the domain name of a legitimate web site. Anyone going to the legitimate site is redirected to an identical but bogus site. Once redirected, unsuspecting site users will enter personal information, such as a password, PIN number or account number.

According a Gartner Study on Internet identity theft, based on a survey of 5000 U.S. adult Internet users, it has been estimated that:

- 1.78 million adults could have fallen victim to the scams
- 57 million adults have experienced a phishing attack
- The cost of phishing… 1.2 billion dollars!

It 'clear that the figures mentioned are a great attraction for criminal organizations that are devoting substantial resources and investments in the sector. An increasing component of organized crime is specializing in this kind of activity characterized by high profits and low risks compared to traditional criminal activities. In the US The Federal Trade Commission is monitoring the phenomenon of Identity Theft with main national agencies promoting several activities to aware the population regarding the risks derived to the crime exposure.

How To Exit The Matrix -And Prevent Identity Theft

When we think to cybercrime we must consider how easy Identity theft in the web has become, so we search for some statistics on a worrying phenomenon and we found data, in each region of the world, similar to the ones we are going to introduce.

1. FBI-related Scams – Scams in which a criminal poses as the FBI to defraud victims.
2. Identity Theft – Unauthorized use of a victim's personal identifying information to commit fraud or other crimes.
3. Advance Fee Fraud – Criminals convince victims to pay a fee to receive something of value, but do not deliver anything of value to the victim.
4. Non-Auction/Non-Delivery of Merchandise -Purchaser does not receive items purchased.
5. Overpayment Fraud – An incident in which the complainant receives an invalid monetary instrument with instructions to deposit it in a bank account and send excess funds or a percentage of the deposited money back to the sender.

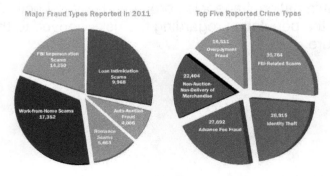

Figure 50 – Crime Statistics from 2011 IC3 Report

These were the top five most common complaints made to the joint FBI/National White Collar Crime Center's Internet Crime Complaint Center (IC3) last year, according to its just-released 2011 Internet Crime Report. Why is this, because as you surf in the web you leave all kinds of information about what sites you visited, what you looked at and your information is being sold, diced and sliced and you have no power to stop it, *or do you*.

What if I was to offer you a way to do your business online and not leave all this information for merchants and criminals?
The ToR -Network is your solution: once inside the matrix/DeepWeb you can still cruise the same Clear Web sites like Amazon and iTunes stores but now with complete anonymity. You are in control of you data more than ever before. It takes a few extra steps, if it was easy everyone would do it but then they would also have total control of their personal data.

Privacy and anonymity have been poop to the point of non-existence in recent years. Our personal, private information is stockpiled and sold to the highest bidder like so much inventory at a warehouse. National Security Letters are written to make countless requests for records from our search engines, libraries, and bookstores with no court oversight. Emails and especially searchable data are practically unprotected from anyone who might ask to have them. All our electronic communications are tapped. Massive governmental data mining schemes are being built to record everything we publish on the web. In many workplaces, employers spy on and control their employees' Internet access, and this practice is widely considered to be acceptable.

The ToR network is a network that provides anonymity (your Identity is safe-secure) were you use it in the **surface web** or the **deep web** or the **dark web** it's up to you, let us remind you that The Dark Web is not the Deep Web.

These are dark times, The Fourth Amendment has all but disappeared, thanks to the Wars on Drugs, Porn, and Terror, in New York they are trying to pass a law to prevent people from commenting online as "anonymous" using the cyber-bully as a way to make everyone give out their personal information before they can post a comment on a website- how the chip at our rights.

Any practicing trial lawyer will tell you that you can no longer rely on unreasonable search to be the basis for excluding evidence, especially for digital evidence in the hands of a third party. Likewise the First Amendment has been shredded with exceptions and provisos, and is only truly available to those with the money to fight costly (and usually frivolous) court battles against large corporations. In short, you can say what you want so long as it doesn't affect corporate profits.

How we got to a legal state where this all this activity is the accepted norm, I'm not quite sure. It seems to stem from an underlying assumption that our function at work and at home is that of a diligent slave, a single unit of economic output under the direct watch and total control of our superiors at all times, we should accept this surveillance because we should have nothing to hide from our benevolent overlords who are watching us merely to protect us from evil.

The Deep Web is not the Tor Network, but you need the ToR network to get to the Dark Web.
The Dark Web is not the Black Market that is a small part of the Dark Web.

Ok, we have gone overboard but there is truth in what we say as others have said before me. Now if we could do something about non-delivery of payment or goods– you can use the ToR-network and not go into the deep web just use the technology to make yourself more secure and have anonymity but surf the clearWeb. If you use the ToR network you can eliminate most of these information leak's and you can have more control of your data– try it, you may like it .

ATM skimming

ATM skimming is proliferating, next to the overall availability of bank plastic cards, holograms and pretty much everything a carder needs to cash out the fraudulently obtained credit card data. From ATM skimmers with Bluetooth notification, to ATM skimmers with SMS notification, what are some of the latest innovations in this field that you're observing? One innovation in skimming that we wrote about recently is that **crooks are starting to turn to 3D Printers to make these devices**. An investigator in California shared with us some photos of what was believed to be a 3D printed skimming device, which was the news hook for that story. But as we were researching the topic, we discovered that a skimmer gang had recently been convicted of creating skimming devices made with a 3D printer they had purchased with the proceeds of their previous skimming crimes.

Pharmaceutical Affiliate Networks

We think there are a few trends emerging, and they all have to do with the fact that it's getting harder for rogue pharmacies to make money. One is a shift toward more generic and herbal medications.

The affiliate programs seem to be looking for drugs to sell that don't incur intellectual property violation cases, which can get them shut down in a hurry. But we think it is becoming much harder for the larger volume spam and scareware affiliate programs out there to retain reliable processing, and that's a long overdue but welcome development.

Eastern Europe is the epicenter of the Cybercrime epidemic

If you mean financially motivated cybercrime that affects the rest of the world, we would say without question hackers in Russia and Eastern Europe are the most active, if not also the most profitable. I think there are cases where (dis)organized crime groups have and are conducting a lot of cybercrimes, but many of these sophisticated groups tend to be regional and stick to attacking their own (Brazil is a good example).

But generally speaking we think it is a mistake to try to measure cybercrime by actual losses, which almost never comes close to the real losses and damage done by cybercrime, costs incurred by software and hardware and personnel defenses, etc. Don't get us wrong: we strongly believe that all nations should be working harder to quantify and publish data about cybercrime losses, particularly in the financial sectors. But the reality is that even some of the most active criminal groups — such as the rogue pharmacy "partnerka" programs like SpamIt and GlavMed and Rx-Promotion — employed some of the biggest botmaster with the biggest botnets, and while some of them made a lot of money, most did not. And the spam "partnerkas" are excellent examples of cases where there are huge asymmetries between their earnings for these activities and the tens of billions of dollars companies and individuals need to spend each year to try to block all of its attendant ills.

Case study - Russian cybercrime, not only a localized threat

Several times we wrote on cybercrime trying to analyze a phenomenon that grows with an impressive rhythm. The trend is uniform all over the word, cybercrime business is increasing its profits despite the economic crisis. The impact of cybercrime is transversal, industry, private businesses and governments, are all players that suffers the incoming cyber threats.

We've found really interesting a research realized by the Russian security firm Group-IB that analyzes the cybercrime activities conducted by the Russian mafia and other criminal organizations.

Group-IB Report :http://go.eset.com/us/resources/white-papers/CARO_2011.pdf

The official estimates says that the global cybercrime market was worth $12.5 billion in 2011, $4,5 billion of the market are related to Russian speaking cybercrime market and $2.3 billion took place in Russia alone. Compared to last years the figures are doubled.
The report provides a clear picture of the cybercrime market providing an interesting perspective on analysis, cybercrime studied as part of a local economies of a region. We are speaking of crime of course but also the crime could have an economic impact on local economies especially for those regions that lives in evident discomfort.

The study highlights key aspects of cybercrime market:
- on line fraud (e.g. online banking fraud, phishing attacks) It should be noted that this aspect includes cashing services for stolen funds, taking up around 40% of this entire aspect.
- spam, including services for sale of drugs and counterfeit products.
- Internal market (cybercrime to cybercrime), including services for anonymization and sale of traffic, exploits, malware, and loaders.
- DDoS attacks

Figure 51 - Infograph on Russian cybercrime

Really interesting the diagram proposed in the report related the economic profit of the activities and the damages to the end users, On-line Spam campaign and banking fraud are the most profitable activities. Due large profits related this

TREND	TOTAL MARKET SHARE	AMOUNT
ONLINE FRAUD		
Online banking fraud	21.3%	490 million $
Cashing	16%	367 million $
Phishing	2.4%	55 million $
Theft of electronic funds	1.3%	30 million $
Total:	41%	942 million $
SPAM		
Spam	24%	553 million $
Pharma and counterfeits	6.2%	142 million $
Fake software	5.9%	135 million $
Total:	36.1%	830 million $
INTERNAL MARKET (C2C)		
Sale of traffic	6.6%	153 million $
Sale of exploits	1.8%	41 million $
Sale of loaders	1.2%	27 million $
Anonymization	0.4%	9 million $
Total:	10%	230 million $
DDOS ATTACKS		
DDoS attacks	5.6%	130 million $
Total:	5.6%	130 million $
OTHER		
Other	7.3%	168 million $
Total:	7.3%	168 million $

crimes security sector is observing a rapid grown of number of incidents.

Figure 52 -On line statistics on cybercrime

The Deep Dark Web – the hidden web

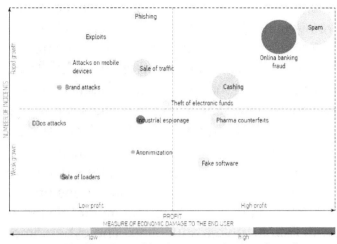

Figure 53 - Number of incidents and related profits

What is really worrying is that the growth of cybercrime activities indicates that the crime is becoming organized, in more than one occasion I have compared crime organization to structured companies that operate with clear objectives and that sustain their affairs. In particular this aspect signs a substantial difference with the past, Russian cybercriminal operations were unorganized and managed by different and not coordinate groups of criminals.

In 2011, the following general trends of cybercrime market development can be highlighted:

- Consolidation of the cybercrime market share, we are assisting to the formation of several major cybercrime groups that differently from the past are setting up in structured organizations.
- Increasing of the activities of collaboration between cybercrime organizations, what we have defined cybercrime to cybercrime business (C2C). The cybercrime is arranging its business in main groups that mutual supports criminal activities such as botnets creation and management and fraud development.

- Infiltration of cybercrime in the social contest, reinvesting the profit of the operations in cyber criminal's activities but also in legal business. The cybercrime is changing, it is merging its structures with the traditional ones, with the subsequent resource allocation from the mafia's areas of control (prostitution, drug and arms trafficking, and so on) in favor of cybercrime. Let's also consider that cybercrime presents the advantages of high profits with relative low risks … usually it goes unpunished.
- Penetration of the cybercrime market by individuals with little technical education. The cybercrime activities mainly require capital investments, not specialized knowledge. The emergence of this trend has led to the expansion of the internal cybercrime market (C2C) and the appearance there of outsourcing services (administration, training, consulting, etc.);
- Growth of the Cybercrime to Cybercrime (C2C) services, provided on a paid basis by specialized teams of hackers.

Actually cybercrime is widespread throughout Russia, many expert have defined the Russian areas the cybercrime heaven, the main reason of the growth of this type of crime in the countries of the former Soviet Union is the absence of an efficient Russian laws that contrast the phenomenon. Russian laws require significant improvements and in my opinion it's not possible to fight against cybercrime without an international cooperation that is a critical aspects because the policy of Moscow Government is closed to external support. The report address another problem, Russia doesn't devote attention to training law enforcement officers and court officials regarding the main issues of IT security, allowing them to make independent judgments on various aspects of cybercrime.

Thus, because of imperfections in Russian laws and the lack of severe penalties, stable law enforcement practice, and regular training regarding counter cybercrime measures, cybercriminals are disproportionately liable for the crimes they commit.

The cybercrime is a cross nations threat and the only way to fight it is the establishment of international laws and with the collaboration of every countries … cybercrime has no borders … the same must be for the measures to prevent it.

Active Malware/Crime ware campaigns:

We think we can continue to expect to see Microsoft doing whatever it can to disrupt cyber criminal activity, because 95 percent of it or more is aimed squarely at their customer base.

Whether the gains from those take downs and targeted actions have long or short-term consequences may not be so important to Microsoft. From our lengthy interviews with Microsoft's chief legal strategist on this subject, it was clear that their first order of business with these actions is raising the costs of doing business for the bad guys, and I think on that front they probably will succeed in the long run if they keep going after them as they are.

Botnet, pro & cons of using Tor Networks

As declared several time Deep Web, thanks to the anonymity of its connection, provides to cyber criminals an ideal environment to grow up profitable business. We have mainly discussed of deep web such as a portion of cyber space mainly used to sell any kind of good, from malware agent to drugs and other criminal services, but the hidden world could also be used to give host to component of a malicious architecture used by cyber criminals.

On September 2012 the German security firm G Data Software has detected a botnet with a particular feature, it is controlled from an Internet Relay Chat (IRC) server running as a hidden service of the Tor.

The Deep Dark Web – the hidden web

I discussed in past article of the advantage of this design choice, let's think for example to how much difficult could be the localization of the command and control servers, due the encryption of the connections interior to the network and the unpredictability of the routing of the information.
The security engineer Dennis Brown during the Defcon Conference in 2010 discussed the possibility of using the Tor network to host botnet command and control servers.
The engineer explained the advantage to adopt an hidden service in a botnet architecture that is summarized in the following points:

- Availability of Authenticated Hidden Services.
- Availability Private Tor Networks
- Possibility of Exit Node Flooding

The mechanism used by IDS is based on the detection of known signatures available for the principal botnet agents, this implies the analysis of the data transmitted by infected machines. In the specific case the traffic is routed is encrypted making hard the process of analysis, let's remind that the hidden services inside the Tor network which can only be accessed from within the Tor network knowing the assigned .onion address.

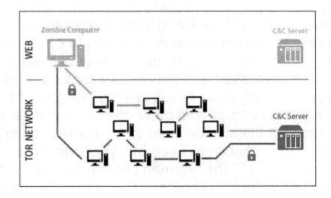

Figure 54 - Botnet based on Tor Network

The model of botnet could be used for various scopes, in military as cyber weapon, in industry for cyber espionage, in cybercrime to steal sensible information such as banking credentials.

Researchers use traffic analysis to detect botnet activities and to localize the control servers, typically Intrusion Detection Systems and network analyzers are adopted for the purpose.

Once detected the botnet to decapitate it are used different methods such as:

- IP of C&C server obscuration
- Cleaning of server hosting botnet and of compromised hosts
- Domain name revoke
- Hosting provider de-peered

The Researcher Dennis Brown proposed a couple of solutions to use Tor network for botnet infrastructure:

1. "Tor2Web proxy based model"
2. "Proxy-aware Malware over Tor network"

"Tor2Web proxy based model"

The use of hidden services for a botnet setup is an interesting choice, an HTTP hidden service could operate behind network devices such as NAT or Firewalls without the need to expose services to the network. The preparation phase of a botnet is quite easy due the large availability of web server easy to setup as hidden service in the DeepWeb and the possibility to retrieve botnet components practically everywhere. Botnet infrastructure are increasing in complexity but are also equipped with friendly administration consoles that make easy their configuration.

In the model proposed the traffic leaves the Tor network using Tor2Web proxy to redirect .onion web traffic, let remind that tor2web is a project to let Internet users access anonymous servers.

"Here's how it works: Imagine you've got something that you want to publish anonymously, like the Federalist Papers or leaked documents from a whistleblower. You publish them via HTTP using a Tor *hidden service; that way your anonymity is protected. Then people access those documents through tor2web; that way anyone with a Web browser can see them."*

The Scripts to run Command and Control happens via Tor2Web so that the bot have to connect to the hidden service passing through the proxy pointing to an address

http://tor2web.org/fiewfh9sfh2fj

In this way the traffic is redirect by the proxy to the Hidden Service identified by an .onion address, the Command & Control servers remain so hidden in the Tor network and are impossible to track down.
The weaknesses aspects of a similar approach are that is normally easy to filter Tor2Web traffic, similar proxy must be managed by botmaster in order to avoid failure or logging from third parts and the entire infrastructures suffer of the considerable latencies of Tor network that make unresponsive a botnet build with this approach.

"Proxy-aware Malware over Tor network"

The second scenario does not provide for Tor2Web, instead it make us of proxy-aware malware, agent that due the absence of Tor2Web have to run Tor on infected hosts. The main difference respect the first solution is in the requirements for the bot agents and their configuration, Bots need to have SOCKS5 support to be able to connect through Tor to .onion addresses loading Tor on the victims.
This second approach is more secure because traffic isn't routed through a proxy and is entirely within Tor network due the direct connection between Bots and C&C, avoiding the possibility to intercept data from exit nodes that are not used for this scenario.

It's clear that a similar approach is more complex from a Bot side, a bot needs SOCKS5 support and of course it need that Tor have to function properly to maintain the synchronization within the machines of the botnet. To presence of Tor traffic on a network may indicate the presence of a similar botnet architecture that can be so detected using network anomaly detection methods.

G Data experts declared

"In other words: Tor tends to be slow and unreliable, and inherits these flaws to underlying botnets."

Our personal opinion is that today is not so difficult to build a bot net based on Tor networks and as declared by researchers the cons of this choice are mainly related to slowness of the network. As usual the best solution is represented by a compromise, similar solution represents a valid choice to maintain hidden the command and control servers making hard the investigations for security experts and law enforcement.
The solutions presented must represent an insight into the topic in order to develop appropriate countermeasures if we were to find us before such botnets.

Cybercrime Ecosystem – Sophisticated Cybercriminals

I consider it a badge of honor that these guys bother to thumb their noses at me. The most recent one I'm aware of was whoever was in charge of coding the Citadel Trojan added some strings in the malware that said, ""Coded by BRIAN KREBS for personal use only. I love my job & wife". Sort of a friendly jab and a vague, nonspecific threat rolled into one. Sometimes it is just kids looking for attention, but by and large I think most of these guys truly resent having any outside light — especially from "amers" or Americans —

shed on their operations. They also don't like it when you distill their operations, norms or processes into bite sized chunks that demystify their ecosystem or forums.

I can't speak for law enforcement activity, but as a journalist and investigative reporter, I'm always sad to see these communities go away. I think it's safe to say that most of them are already infiltrated by several national law enforcement organizations. I'd be very surprised if they were not. Some operating right now probably were even set up by law enforcement. We've seen them do that a few times before. I think most of the fraudsters who've been doing this long enough probably understand that and act accordingly. Others do not, and that is why you tend to see lots of people come and go, but the same core group of a few hundred guys are the top dogs on most important forums.

Communities and crime forums are great places to learn intelligence about upcoming and ongoing attacks, breaches, 0days, etc. Shutting them down seems to me to be counterproductive, since you almost always force the forums to go more underground and use more security features to keep un-trusted people out, and known sources of intelligence go away, or worse yet change their nicks and contact info and all of a sudden a source you have developed you may never see or hear from again.

Risk-forwarding cybercrime ecosystem

The rise of money mule recruitment

We've identified quite a few distinct money mule recruitment networks. We don't know about templates, but many of them tend to recycle the same HMTL content and change the names of the fake companies. That's handy we guess for keeping track of which group recruited which mules, but beyond that we are not sure it tells you much. What we have noticed is that money mules are the bottleneck for this type of fraud, and often times the cyber crooks will leave money in the victim's account because they simply didn't have enough mules to help them haul all of the loot. So with any one victim, it's typical to find mules recruited through 4-6 different mule recruitment gangs, because the fraudsters who outsource this recruitment will simply go from one to the other purchasing the services of these recruitment gangs until they've got enough to help them haul the loot, or they've exhausted the available mule supply. But usually, the mule gangs don't have any problem finding new recruits.

Are **reshipping mules** more popular than **money mules**

We think reshipping mules tend to be more useful. Most regular money mules are one-and-done. They're used for a single task and then discarded (although one group we are following re-uses money mules as many times as they can before the mule starts to ask for their monthly salary). Typically, a reshipping gang will get 3-5 packages reshipped per weekday per mule, and the average reshipping mule works for 30 days before figuring out they've been working for free and great personal risk and they're never going to get paid, or the check they got from their employer just bounced.

But several mule gangs we are aware of do both reshipping and money mules interchangeably.

Online gambling

Advanced persistent threats (APT attacks)

We think if there has been a net positive about the shift in focus (at least from the mainstream security industry) away from traditional threats to APT attacks it is in the increased attention paid to social engineering attacks, which form the basis of most successful attacks today. 0-day threats get a lot of press and are frequently associated with APT attacks, but it is far more common for these attacks to leverage known vulnerabilities for which there are patches, much like exploit packs that are used in many Zeus attacks and other more traditional cyber crimes. Unfortunately, educating users about what not to click on or trust or open is always an uphill battle. There are some things that companies could be doing more on this front, and we'd like to see more firms randomly test their employees to help speed the process of learning how not to fall for phishing and social engineering scams.

Scareware industry, scareware remains one of the most profitable monetization strategies within the cybercrime ecosystem

We don't think scareware is the same scourge it used to be, although it's clearly still a problem. We would say this problem — like the pharmacy spam problem — must be attacked at the payment processing point; that is where it makes the most sense. There are some things afoot in the payment processing space that I think will probably start to show major results in the coming months on this front, but the proof will be when the scareware partner programs start dying off completely because the business model has dried up. We think we can expect to see the costs of acquiring banks taking on this business continue to rise, and that will help make the scareware industry less profitable and less attractive for scammers.

Migration of cybercrime from clear web to the deep web

We all remember the Citadel Trojan, based on the Zeus experience has evolved becoming one of the most interesting cyber criminal project. Few months ago we wrote on the excellent customer relationship management (CRM) model implemented by its creators. Thanks a malware evolution dictated by market needs, the Trojan has evolved in time, many instances have been detected with different powerful features developed for specific clients. The creators of the agent have structured an efficient services for the sell (with sales price of nearly $2,500) and the supply of improvement services for the Trojan through social network platforms.
But just one of the strengths of the model, the opportunity to get in touch with the creators of the virus, paradoxically, could stop the spread of the dreaded malware.

So how to protect anonymity of the creators maintaining a malware as service selling model?
Deep web gives a great opportunity, that's why Citadel's authors will probably migrate to the hidden web, trying to avoid the controls of law enforcement.

Figure 55 - Citadel admin panel

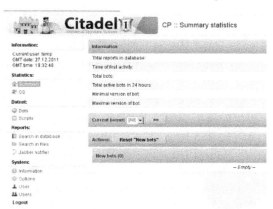

The need to restrict the audience of prospective customers could restrict the global business preserving its vitality. Another threat to the Citadel's model is represented by the researchers that could infiltrate the customer's networks to reverse engine the instances of malware to neutralize them. Recently the security blog S21Sec discovered a new version of Citadel developed to avoid detection and analysis usually done using sandboxes.
Very interesting the discovery of a specific anti-emulator, which allows to protect botnet from reversing engineering and being tracked. Once started the component is able to detect if the malware is running in a virtual environment (e.g. VMware, Virtualbox) and in that case to implement hiding techniques to avoid the detecting of the Trojan.
The anonymity is the need for cyber criminal, we have assisted to the proliferation of encrypted instant messaging communications and of VPN service providers, all to avoid to be spied on.

The Deep Dark Web – the hidden web

Cyber crime is characterized by a technical soul that is pushing the implementation of new hidden services deployed in the dark web.

New specific figures are emerging, cyber experts that are able to setup efficient market services far from the eyes of law enforcement.

We are assisting to the consolidation of the black market, brokers can set up auctions to sell new malware and zero-day vulnerabilities ensuring the anonymity of the parties.

We are assisting to a massive movement of the malware market from the clear web to the deep web, specific services are multiplying in network such as Freenet and Tor.

Following cyber criminals in deep web is much harder, tracking activities are essentially possible due the infiltration of agents, but it's not so simple. These new dark communities they are increasingly becoming closed, they are elusive and difficult to locate.

It the deep web is quite simple to find any kind of services that sells every type of odds such as drugs, weapons, credit cards and so on, a market without rules, with a unique imperative .... make money.

Living in the deep web with conviction that it can offer a kind of immunity to crime is deeply wrong, technological methods and infiltration make in the time are the winning. Consider that for example law enforcement all over the world maintains a set of fake identities during the years to infiltrate forums, they work in active way proposing solutions or making trade of fraudulent goods.

One of the phenomena that more is benefiting for the movement of the cg of illegal market from clear web to deep web has been identifies has cybercrime-as-a-service, a new model of Cybercrime to cybercrime (C2C) where ordinary crime meets the offer of cyber criminal to prepare cyber attacks or cyber frauds without having technical knowledge.

Cyber criminal organizations operate as enterprise, last week we have read about the Capfire4 service that proposes tools for the organization of cyber attacks such as spam of malware, malware hosting, and a to build up a complete command and control infrastructure (C&C) for the arrangement of botnets.

Similar service is really efficient but to noisy, law enforcement and also security press have immediately localized it, due this reason the crime is emigrating in that part of web not indexable by common search engines.

What to expect from the future?
From technological point of view, the use of the deep web is the best choice, the right balance between openness of the business and anonymity.

The crime industries evolved, following the technological solutions proposed by IT leading enterprises, and at least in the computer industry, it has set up a proven and extremely efficient model of sales and CRM.

The persecution of this type of crime is complex for a multitude of factors, both on the legislative and technological perspective.

Surely there is much to do today in an attempt to infiltrate these emerging organizations, often lack a consolidated background also due young age of gang members and therefore vulnerable to external influences.

Another critical aspect in the tracking of these activities is related to the circulation of money and problems relating to payments, we discussed about BitCoin and services for the anonymity of the transfers, though to date precisely this phase is the most critical for those who want to make criminal profits without being traced.

The only certainty is the need to define a suitable model for investigations in an area that is explored relatively recently.

Digging in the Silk Road, study of the famous market places

The Deep Dark Web – the hidden web

Yes Guys, when we think to the deep web the media tell us only about its dark side, it's considered the paradise of cybercrime, the reign of the theft, a place to escape, but is it true?

The governments want you stay far from hidden web, because they cannot spy on you, the crime is in deep web as in the clear web and we have described it in detail in the incoming Book, the "Deep Dark Web".

Of course the anonymity granted by deep web could encourage and facilitate criminal activities but at same time it represent an obstacle to the criminal that for example desire to steal sensible information of the users or spy on them.

Meanwhile on the clear web we are able to find many reports produced by security firms on cyber criminal activities and related earnings, we know relatively little about the profits related to the Deep Web that we remember to be of size and turnover dramatically greater than the dark web.

I've found an interesting research made by the Carnegie Mellon computer security professor Nicolas Christin on the earning of one of the most famous black market in the deep web, Silk Road, that seems to be able to realize $22 Million In Annual Sales only related to the drug market. Total revenue made by the sellers has been estimated around USD 1.9 million per month, an incredible business also for the Silk Road operators that receive about USD 143,000 per month in commissions.

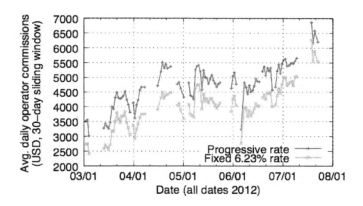

Figure 56 – Silk Road Avg. daily operator commissions

The experts have examined over 24,400 separate items sold on the popular site demonstrating that Silk Road is mainly used as drugs market, very interesting also the composition of the sellers that for obvious needs leaves within a couple of weeks the site to appear in second time.

The study highlights that the famous market reach $22 million in annual sales and around double the commission respect six months ago.

First of all where is located Silk Road?

Silk Road is an hidden service exposed, be aware hidden service doesn't mean that it's difficult to locate but this is the meaning that is used for the service provided in the anonymizing network for the reason that I explained in the past articles on the subject.

We are facing with a complex economy that has also its electronic currency, the Bitcoin, another argument that we have already introduced. We can consider the market armored due the anonymity mechanisms that it trade on, from the Tor Network to the payment methods.

The study has analyzed the evolution of the market in the last months demonstrating the increasing of the business may be obtained also thanks to the aura of mystery that many media give the Deep Web.

The number of sellers of any kind of drugs is passed from 300 in February to around 570 in August as reported in the following graph:

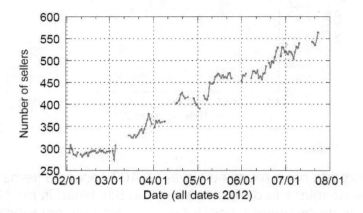

Figure 57 - Silk Road N° of sellers during the study

The analysis have been conducted running crawler program against the website and at same time monitoring the activities of the site administrator to understand if the study was intercepted.
The researchers have participated to the forum of the site without noting any signal that demonstrated that there crawler were discovered.

The application used for the analysis were able to collect any kind of information related to the product sold such as pricing information and feedbacks posted by the buyer (surprisingly high level of customer satisfaction, around 97.8%), an useful information to estimate the number of sales.
To avoid detection of measurements the team has used different Tor circuits and have performed analysis randomly during every day.

Which are the most sold products?

The study has grouped the product in categories and has revealed that the "most wanted" items are drugs, following is proposed the list of the Top 20 categories in terms of items available.

Category	#. items	Pct.
Weed	3338	13.7%
Drugs	2207	9.0%
Prescription	1784	7.3%
Benzos	1193	4.9%
Books	955	3.9%
Cannabis	880	3.6%
Hash	821	3.4%
Cocaine	633	2.6%
Pills	473	1.9%
Blotter	441	1.8%
Money	406	1.7%
MDMA (ecstasy)	393	1.6%
Erotica	385	1.6%
Steroids, PEDs	376	1.5%
Seeds	375	1.5%
Heroin	370	1.5%
Opioids	344	1.4%
DMT	343	1.4%
Stimulants	292	1.2%
Digital goods	261	1.1%

Figure 59 - N° items per categories

Figure 58 - Top 20 (

The study has also tried to take a picture of typical seller, of course excluding its identity that is impossible (maybe ;-)) to track. First, we specify that due to the anonymous nature of the market place, it is impossible to discern whether certain sellers use multiple seller pages, we can only speculate that a seller will use for convenience a single page to prost its product.

Most sellers leave the site fairly quickly, but a core of about 4% of them have been on the site for the entire duration of our study, the majority of sellers are only on the site for less than two months, may be because they leave the site once sold the products or because they move "into stealth mode as soon as they have established a large enough customer base".

Another interesting data is related to the location of the sellers and buyer, information that has been obtained from the list of acceptable shipping destinations of the items. The following table 2 shows the top 12 locations for both origin

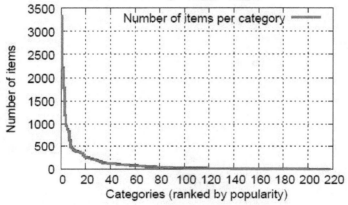

and destinations. Most items ship from the United States, with the United Kingdom a distant second and The Netherlands where the government permits narcotics sales.

The study reveals that a majority of items ship worldwide, in

Origin		Acceptable destinations	
Country	Pct.	Country/Region	Pct.
U.S.A.	43.86%	Worldwide	49.70%
Undeclared	16.28%	U.S.A.	35.13%
U.K.	10.14%	European Union	6.19%
Netherlands	6.51%	Canada	6.04%
Canada	5.91%	U.K.	3.65%
Germany	4.50%	Australia	2.87%
Australia	3.19%	World. excpt. U.S.A.	1.39%
India	1.22%	Germany	1.03%
Italy	1.02%	Norway	0.70%
China	0.97%	Switzerland	0.61%
Spain	0.93%	New Zealand	0.57%
France	0.82%	Undeclared	0.26%

spite of the nature of the items, considering that the odds are paid only once received and that the quantities being sold are generally .... Figure 60 - Top Origin and Acceptable destinations of Silk r sellers use techniques to make package inspection unlikely, for example using vacuum sealing and of course a "professional-looking" envelopes with typed destination addresses. In this way it's hard to trace the senders because they also use private couriers to ship the items. Giving a look to the economic aspects of the market we must consider first that all transactions are using Bitcoin currency that is a notoriously volatile currency. Analyzing the evolution of the exchange rate of the Bitcoin against the three major currencies that sellers use in their countries, is possible to note that the Bitcoin exchange rate has remained relatively stable between the end of February and early May, oscillating around 1 BTCUSD 5, and corresponding values in Euros and pounds. Since then, the Bitcoin has notably appreciated, reaching close to USD 9 since mid-July 2012, with relatively large fluctuations in value. The evolution of product prices closely mirrors the evolution of the Bitcoin exchange rates suggesting little inflation for these items over the time interval considered.

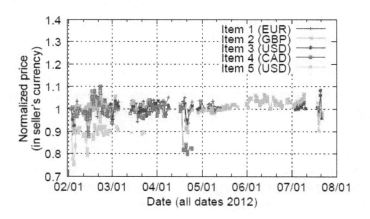

Figure 61 - Product Normalized price in seller's currency

Reflections

The experts and law enforcement are conscious that are facing with an anomalous market where identities are hidden, payments difficult to trace, where no advertising is made and where the access to the "market place" implies anonymizing tool such as a Tor client. Despite all this consideration the study has revealed a string growth of the business, the market appears in expansion and number of sellers that use it is dramatically increased. Christin declared

"It's a stable marketplace, and overall it's growing steadily."

But many users on the site have worried for possible infiltration made by law enforcement, another source of concerns is that several of its high-profile sellers have disappeared.

The possibility to infiltrate a similar market is concrete and market place such as Silk Road represents in my opinion a moderate risks for the worldwide community. The most problematic aspects of similar business is that they are controlled by criminal organization but the figure proposed are far from to justify a massive Government intervention, the problem is how much hidden services like this are in the hidden web?

I believe that government are working on the possibility also to fight this type of cybercrimes but are worried by most dangerous way to use anonymizing networks.

In the reports are also proposed some solution to stop the market place, some of them really impractical like the block of Tor networks, don't forget that government primary use this type of networks that they have designed and promoted ...

Are market place such as Silk Road an acceptable side effect?

Terrorist

Monitoring Cyber Iran And Syria In The Tor Network

We were monitoring bad ToR-Relays and found that during this unrest in Iran and Syria. We have 17 bad ToR-Relays 95% in Iran and Syria. This is how the shut down the network to suppress information communication securely to the outside world. *Time stamp is 05-31-2012 00:52:05* MET. Tor Network Status – *http://torstatus.blutmagie.de/index.php* you can find all kinds of information about the .onion relays that make up the networks. While back in cyber world — :Stuxnet – Flame – we can tell you that lot's of Iranian site use older web apps , cms, jommla and they have vulnerabilities.

Iran Sites Open 2 Joomla -K-CMS Hacking - http://uscyberlabs.com/blog/2012/02/10/1890/

But they are educated and everyone learns from being attacked. When you underestimate your enemy you are going to lose.

Example : I been working on a ToR project and last night I was monitoring the ToR-Relays for bad ones and 15 out of 17 -ToR-Relays all doing exit node were Iranian and Syrians all bad and compromised. With the unrest in the news with Iran and Syria these two countries were playing with Tor-Relay nodes to extract exit information on dissidents. If they catch some dissident posting anti-Iran, anti-Syria online and they will find their IP and kill them. In the middle east Hacktivist may pay the ultimate price and the CIA and others are communicating with the rebels using the ToR-.onion network the invisible web takes on a new importance during crisis time.

All goes underground under the radar but it shows that they have an active cyber policy, with countermeasure and surveillance. These guy are fighting back anyway they can. Cyber and culture must be understood, the more you invest in your infrastructure the more vulnerable you will become and how a society integrates the technology into it's culture will make changes, trust me business will love it but in the middle east religion is very important geo-political tool and propaganda is the number one thing I see while surfing the Iran. Syria websites.

Today I see "cyber ambiguity" from Israel –On Tuesday, a day after a Moscow based security company revealed that a new cyber weapon called "Flame" had struck Iran, Vice Premier and Minister of Strategic Affairs Moshe Ya'alon fueled speculation of Israeli involvement by praising Israeli technological prowess in response to a radio interview on the issue.

Israel, he said, was blessed with superior technology.
"These achievements of ours open all kinds of possibilities for us," he said.

Prime Minister Binyamin Netanyahu said when he spoke that evening that when it comes to cyberspace, the size of a country is insignificant – but that there is great significance to a country's "scientific strength, and with that Israel is blessed."

http://www.jpost.com/Features/FrontLines/Article.aspx?id=27
2264

As all these state actor play cyber games with cyber war, *we* will keep monitoring the ToR network to look and see and learn about societies in cyberspace.

Technical Side – Geeky Side

Technologies used in the Hidden Service

Attacking a ToR .network

We found that there are a few ways to attack a secure network some is old fashion technology and some more modern. The FBI and Secret Service and other international law enforcement have used these technique and they have been de-classified:

UPDATE: -5-21-2012 -0900 There are few more attack vectors that I recently found in the .onion network – let's just say attack from within that – If you are a legit-legal Security Researcher please write me. I want to keep those secret for now –

Let's take a look at:

The Cold Boot Attacks

One of the problems with encryption is that in order for it to work, your computer has to know the private key and any other information needed for decryption. This **information is stored in memory** and while memory isn't a good place to store things long term, it does store data for an amount of time from seconds to minutes after your machine has been turned off. An adversary, knowing that they are facing a locked down machine with lots of encryption, may perform a cold boot attack. This involves **turning off your computer, spraying your memory with liquid nitrogen (or something to keep it cold), and then recovering your encryption key from memory**. Once frozen, data in memory can be retained (and then further reconstructed) for hours.

Countermeasures: *If you feel this is a risk, you need to implement physical security measures that deal with the possible threat. This could be as simple as a laser tripwire on a door that triggers a shutdown.*

Radio Leakage, TEMPEST, etc.

All electronics **create radio interference** as a consequence of their operation. While this radio interference is often useless it can also provide **valuable information for your adversary**. For instance, the radio interference generated by keyboards can divulge your passwords to an adversary sitting across the street from your house. RF shielding is the only solution for this problem and involves surrounding your machine in some type of metal. This isn't all though, as the power pull generated when you use the keyboard, etc. can also be monitored through your wall socket. I don't know of any solutions to this. One idea would be to lock your machine in a box with a UPS to filter the electricity and a security scheme similar to the one used to prevent cold boot attacks but I'm not sure how effective this would be.
Countermeasures: Get some chicken wire and build a faraday cage for all your secure computing equipment. What ever music you like play it loud I would suggest Metal this is filled with so many harmonics that it will very hard to extract the EMF.

Physical Security

An **adversary may put a camera**, microphone, or some other recording device in the room with your hidden service machine. If they capture your encryption passphrase, your data will be compromised. Recently the **FBI and Secret Service used this technique** against a bust of the **ShadowCrew** carding board and it's been used for a long time by both law enforcement and intelligence. While using a blanket will deter a camera, the audio generated by your keyboard may not be sufficiently muffled to stop a microphone from knowing what's going on.
Countermeasures: Always be careful of anyone coming into the place were your computing equipment or office. Remember that today's technology has WiFi cameras and all kinds of devices. Also check you router to see any weird connections to it and remember the logs they will show failed attempts to access your network. Another way is to scan for SSID with Kismet or NetStumbler you may be able to scan

for the device. And for microphones : What ever music you like play it loud I would suggest Metal this is filled with so many harmonics that it will very hard to extract the from the noise.

Traffic Correlation
If your adversary suspects you run a hidden service, they can watch your internet connection and try to use traffic analysis to determine if the hidden service is run on your network. If your adversary downloads a few 50 megabyte files from your server and every time around 50MB of encrypted traffic goes across your network, it's pretty good evidence. Combine that with shutting off the power to your machine and watching the hidden service go down and you've got somebody who knows what's going on.
Countermeasures: *There are creative ways of dealing with this such as cover traffic, UPSs, redundant servers, and physical security.*
a government censor can render it moot by simply blocking the relays

gAtO hopes that this will help you understand that the ToR network a little better and don't worry the Tor Project is working hard on Traffic Correlation attacks. – gAtO oUt

Tor Passive- Active -Directory Attacks on onion network
Passive attacks
Observing user traffic patterns. Observing a user's connection will not reveal her destination or data, but it will reveal traffic patterns (both sent and received). Profiling via user connection patterns requires further processing, because multiple application streams may be operating simultaneously or in series over a single circuit.
Observing user content.
While content at the user end is encrypted, connections to responders may not be (indeed, the responding website itself may be hostile). While filtering content is not a primary goal of Onion Routing, Tor can directly use Privoxy and

related filtering services to anonymize application data streams.

Option distinguishability.
We allow clients to choose configuration options. For example, clients concerned about request linkability should rotate circuits more often than those concerned about traceability. Allowing choice may attract users with different needs; but clients who are in the minority may lose more anonymity by appearing distinct than they gain by optimizing their behavior [1].

End-to-end timing correlation.
Tor only minimally hides such correlations. An attacker watching patterns of traffic at the initiator and the responder will be able to confirm the correspondence with high probability. The greatest protection currently available against such confirmation is to hide the connection between the onion proxy and the first Tor node, by running the OP on the Tor node or behind a firewall. This approach requires an observer to separate traffic originating at the onion router from traffic passing through it: a global observer can do this, but it might be beyond a limited observer's capabilities.

End-to-end size correlation.
Simple packet counting will also be effective in confirming endpoints of a stream. However, even without padding, we may have some limited protection: the leaky pipe topology means different numbers of packets may enter one end of a circuit than exit at the other.

Website fingerprinting.
All the effective passive attacks above are traffic confirmation attacks, which puts them outside our design goals. There is also a passive traffic analysis attack that is potentially effective. Rather than searching exit connections for timing and volume correlations, the adversary may build up a database of "fingerprints" containing file sizes and access patterns for targeted websites. He can later confirm a user's connection to a given site simply by consulting the

database. This attack has been shown to be effective against SafeWeb [29]. It may be less effective against Tor, since streams are multiplexed within the same circuit, and fingerprinting will be limited to the granularity of cells (currently 512 bytes). Additional defenses could include larger cell sizes, padding schemes to group websites into large sets, and link padding or long-range dummies.4

Active attacks
Compromise keys.
An attacker who learns the TLS session key can see control cells and encrypted relay cells on every circuit on that connection; learning a circuit session key lets him unwrap one layer
of the encryption. An attacker who learns an OR's TLS private key can impersonate that OR for the TLS key's lifetime, but he must also learn the onion key to decrypt *create* cells (and because of perfect forward secrecy, he cannot hijack already established circuits without also compromising their session keys). Periodic key rotation limits the window of opportunity for these attacks. On the other hand, an attacker who learns a node's identity key can replace that node indefinitely by sending new forged descriptors to the directory servers.

Iterated compromise.
A roving adversary who can compromise ORs (by system intrusion, legal coercion, or extralegal coercion) could march down the circuit compromising the nodes until he reaches the end. Unless the adversary can complete this attack within the lifetime of the circuit, however, the ORs will have discarded the necessary information before the attack can be completed. (Thanks to the perfect forward secrecy of session keys, the attacker cannot force nodes to decrypt recorded traffic once the circuits have been closed.) Additionally, building circuits that cross jurisdictions can make legal coercion harder—this phenomenon is commonly called "jurisdictional arbitrage." The Java Anon Proxy project recently experienced the need for this approach, when a

German court forced them to add a backdoor to their nodes [51].

Run a recipient.
An adversary running a webserver trivially learns the timing patterns of users connecting to it, and can introduce arbitrary patterns in its responses. End-to-end attacks become easier: if the adversary can induce users to connect to his webserver (perhaps by advertising content targeted to those users), he now holds one end of their connection. There is also a danger that application protocols and associated programs can be induced to reveal information about the initiator. Tor depends on Privoxy and similar protocol cleaners to solve this latter problem.

Run an onion proxy.
It is expected that end users will nearly always run their own local onion proxy. However, in some settings, it may be necessary for the proxy to run remotely— typically, in institutions that want to monitor the activity of those connecting to the proxy. Compromising an onion proxy compromises all future connections through it.

DoS non-observed nodes.
An observer who can only watch some of the Tor network can increase the value of this traffic by attacking non-observed nodes to shut them down, reduce their reliability, or persuade users that they are not trustworthy. The best defense here is robustness.

Run a hostile OR.
In addition to being a local observer, an isolated hostile node can create circuits through itself, or alter traffic patterns to affect traffic at other nodes. Nonetheless, a hostile node must be immediately adjacent to both endpoints to compromise the anonymity of a circuit.
If an adversary can run multiple ORs, and can persuade the directory servers that those ORs are trustworthy and independent, then occasionally some user will choose one of those ORs for the start and another as the end of a circuit. If an adversary controls m > 1 of N nodes, he can correlate at most ($[\mathbf{m/N}]$)**2** of the traffic— although an adversary could still attract a disproportionately large amount of traffic by running an OR with a permissive exit policy, or by degrading the reliability of other routers.

Introduce timing into messages.
This is simply a stronger version of passive timing attacks already discussed earlier.

Tagging attacks.

A hostile node could "tag" a cell by altering it. If the stream were, for example, an unencrypted request to a Web site, the garbled content coming out at the appropriate time would confirm the association. However, integrity checks on cells prevent this attack. *Replace contents of unauthenticated protocols.* When relaying an unauthenticated protocol like HTTP, a hostile exit node can impersonate the target server. Clients should prefer protocols with end-to-end authentication.

Replay attacks.
Some anonymity protocols are vulnerable to replay attacks. Tor is not; replaying one side of a handshake will result in a different negotiated session key, and so the rest of the recorded session can't be used.

Smear attacks.
An attacker could use the Tor network for socially disapproved acts, to bring the network into disrepute and get its operators to shut it down. Exit policies reduce the possibilities for abuse, but ultimately the network requires volunteers who can tolerate some political heat.

Distribute hostile code.
An attacker could trick users into running subverted Tor software that did not, in fact, anonymize their connections—or worse, could trick ORs into running weakened software that provided users with less anonymity. We address this problem (but do not solve it completely) by signing all Tor releases with an official public key, and including an entry in the directory that lists which versions are currently believed to be secure. To prevent an attacker from subverting the official release itself (through threats, bribery, or insider attacks), we provide all releases in source code form, encourage source audits, and frequently warn our users never to trust any software (even from us) that comes without source.

Directory attacks

Destroy directory servers.
If a few directory servers disappear, the others still decide on a valid directory. So long as any directory servers remain in operation, they will still broadcast their views of the network and generate a consensus directory. (If more than half are destroyed, this directory will not, however, have enough signatures for clients to use it automatically; human intervention will be necessary for clients to decide whether to trust the resulting directory.)

Subvert a directory server.
By taking over a directory server, an attacker can partially influence the final directory. Since ORs are included or excluded by majority vote, the corrupt directory can at worst cast a tie-breaking vote to decide whether to include marginal ORs. It remains to be seen how often such marginal cases occur in practice. *Subvert a majority of directory servers.* An adversary who controls more than half the directory servers can include as many compromised ORs in the final directory as he wishes. We must ensure that directory server operators are independent and attack-resistant.

Encourage directory server dissent.
The directory agreement protocol assumes that directory server operators agree on the set of directory servers. An adversary who can persuade some of the directory server operators to distrust one another could split the quorum into mutually hostile camps, thus partitioning users based on which directory they use. Tor does not address this attack.

Trick the directory servers into listing a hostile OR.
Our threat model explicitly assumes directory server operators will be able to filter out most hostile ORs.

Convince the directories that a malfunctioning OR is working.

In the current Tor implementation, directory servers assume that an OR is running correctly if they can start a TLS connection to it. A hostile OR could easily subvert this test by accepting TLS connections from ORs but ignoring all cells. Directory servers must actively test ORs by building circuits and streams as appropriate. The tradeoffs of a similar approach are discussed in deny Bob service by flooding his introduction points with requests. Because the introduction points can block requests that lack authorization tokens, however, Bob can restrict the volume of requests he receives, or require a certain amount of computation for every request he receives.

Attack an introduction point.
An attacker could disrupt a location-hidden service by disabling its introduction points. But because a service's identity is attached to its public key, the service can simply re-advertise itself at a different introduction point. Advertisements can also be done secretly so that only high-priority clients know the address of Bob's introduction points or so that different clients know of different introduction points. This forces the attacker to disable all possible introduction points.

Compromise an introduction point.
An attacker who controls Bob's introduction point can flood Bob with introduction requests, or prevent valid introduction requests from reaching him. Bob can notice a flood, and close the circuit. To notice blocking of valid requests, however, he should periodically test the introduction point by sending rendezvous requests and making sure he receives them.

Compromise a rendezvous point.
A rendezvous point is no more sensitive than any other OR on a circuit, since all data passing through the rendezvous is encrypted with a session key shared by Alice and Bob.

ToR Relays Monitoring

Cyber Intelligence Monitor Tor Network Services – Live

We wanted -to find a way to gather cyber intelligence on the ToR network you know how and who is using it, the status of the relays that provide you with your security and anonymity. We can see users by countries the User Metric port.

We can monitor ToR relays by countries, relays with exit, fast, guard and stable flags, also the relay version and platform all in one age view. This is remarkable power to monitor events in the OnionLand environment. One feature we love is to monitor by languages lake Farsi and Chinese or English this will give you a history of the usage by culture and events.

We can build a model of all these parameters to monitor the deepWeb. If the deepWeb is so secretive where are these tools in the clearWeb? Now there are hidden ToR-relays but

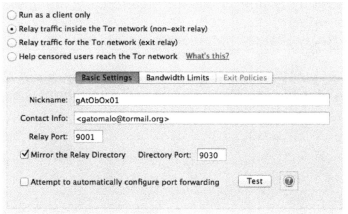

we will talk about those later.

Figure 62 - Relay monitoring

Simplified Chinese zh_CN
In the clear Web everybody knows everything in the deepWeb only the few know it and anonymity. Maybe there is more transparency in the darkWeb that we it give credit the tor-citizens are creating a new world with its own rules. The reason you can't find the good stuff is you don't know how to look.
If it was easy everyone would be doing it. If you want OnionLand cyber intelligence try these sites they may provide some of the clues to the deepWeb, the following site are available in the clearWeb:

Web Site	Address
Tor Network Status	http://torstatus.blutmagie.de/
ToR Metric Portal – Users	https://metrics.torproject.org/users.html
ToR Relay Status Live –Atlas	https://atlas.torproject.org/#search/anony
Tor Relay Status	http://torstatus.all.de/

In the clear Web everybody knows everything in the deepWeb only the few know it and anonymity.

Tor-Relay (OR) Inspector -information about ToR-Relays

We are happy to have found the ToR Inspector site in the .onion. This site has information about all ToR-Relays around the world and it indicates if this ToR-Relay is BAD-GOOD-ERROR-REJECT status. Let's say that you are planning an adventure into ToR land the (*paranoid security - **techy-talk***) thing about ToR that you have to remember is

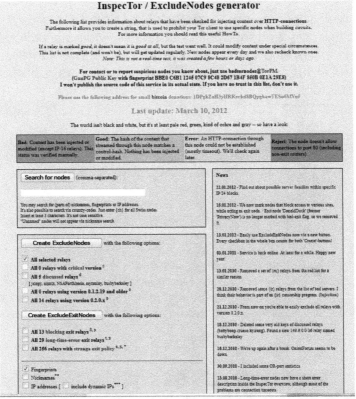

the Entry Node into ToR and the Exit Relay out of ToR. ToR-the .Onion is legal.

ToR security: When you go into ToR the .onion your computer must enter the -ToR-Matrix- so the first ToR-Relay is your entry point and when you leave the .onion your Exit-

Relay is logged by your ISP. **All they know is that you went into ToR and you left. They don't know anything about your session in the deepWeb**. Using the ToR network is not illegal so far today anywhere. In places like the middle east and China it's becoming a problem for these governments so they try mess with the ToR-Relays all the time. On this site [1] **ToR Relay Inspector** you can see if your entry and exit -TOR-Relays are working good and have not been compromised.

The web site provide a comfortable console to search a specific relay and inspect its status providing a collection of useful information such as IP address, Router Details, Version-Platform and other Tor-Relay data as reported in the next picture.

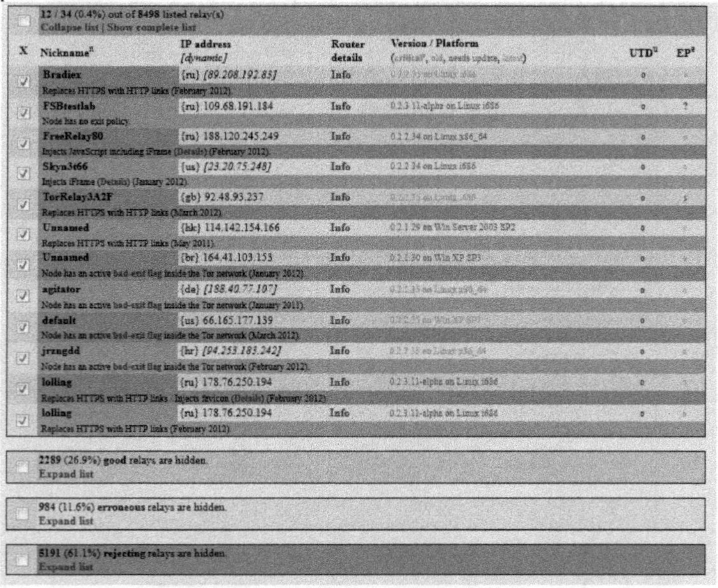

Figure 64 - Relay Status Table

Another powerful site available in the clear web is Blutmagie http://torstatus.blutmagie.de/ that provides a list of Tor Relays very detailed and gives users the ability to perform custom queries, analyzing for example the Tor server located in each country end precious related info such as OS platform, let's think of it as Patch-management on the fly.

Figure 65 - Blutmagie List ot Relays

Following another image related to a specific server:

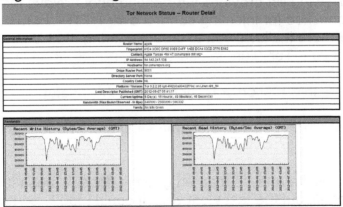

Figure 66 - Blutmagie Relay Detail Form

Now that we know all this information about ToR-Relay we may want to be active and select our own Entry-Exit ToR-Relay, on this page we can create an exclude-Entry-&-Exit-Node so when we can tell our ToR connection what to use. In a place like China were the government is always bring to find and corrupt ToR-Relays this is a great tool.

As security people we need to look at this project which is Donation Only funding and help them. The DeepWeb is open just like Pandora the masses are exploring it and once they feel free and safe it may help them just like it did in the Arab Spring.

We know the deepWeb is being used by the bad guy's too but just like a tool. With a hammer you can build a house or use it to kill a person. This is a good page for any Security Researcher to learn but some bad things are we can see the IP of all the Relays and maybe we can now do a DDoS attack to keep that Relays down – A government can use this tool to see every ToR-Relay in their country and DDoS them, maybe-*sl-nO*.

InspecTor / ExcludeNodes generator
[1] http://xqz3u5drneuzhaeo.onion/users/badtornodes/

The following list provides information about relays that have been checked for injecting content over HTTP-connections. Furthermore it allows you to create a string, that is used to prohibit your Tor client to use specific nodes when building circuits.
For more information you should read this useful How-To.

http://xqz3u5drneuzhaeo.onion/users/badtornodes/howto.ht ml

Be aware, if a relay is marked *good*, it doesn't mean it is *good at all*, but the test went well. It could modify content under special circumstances. This list is not complete (and won't be), but will get updated regularly. New nodes appear every day and we also recheck known ones.

Note: This is not a real-time test, it was created a few hours or days ago.

For contact or to report suspicious nodes you know about, just use badtornodes@TorPM.

(GnuPG Public Key with fingerprint BBE0 C6B1 1245 07C9 8C48 2D67 1B4F 850B 0E1A 29E8)
I won't publish the source code of this service in its actual state. If you have no trust in this list, don't use it.

Tor Metrics

How to use Tor Metrics to discover censorship
Cyber intelligence units are working to develop tools and applications for a deep inspection of the hidden web with the intent of steal classified secret documents of a potential adversary and to maintain the control over cybercrime and terrorists activities and communications.
Let's start from the beginning, which are the available metrics to analyze the status of TOR networks?
The Tor Metrics Portal gives a set of useful the instruments to monitors the workload of the TOR networks, it proposes a complete collection of tools and documentations for statistical analysis regarding the activities of relays and bridges.
The main areas covered by the metrics are:

- statistics on the network of relays and bridges
- statistics on the number of users accessing to the network
- statistics on the number of packages requested from GetTor
- collection of active and passive performance measurements of the Tor network

As we will demonstrate the metrics could also be used for intelligence purpose, for example analyzing principal network metrics it is possible to investigate on the application of monitoring system inside a country for censorship purpose. Recently in many area of the planet similar systems have been used to suppress media protest and to persecute dissidents, avoiding the circulation of unconformable information outside the country. It is happened for example in Syria and in Iran, country where the control of the web is a major concern of the government. These situations are expression of a political sufferance of a country and could give a further element of evaluation to the analysts.

Network of relays and bridges

Tor protects users against traffic analysis using a network of onion routers (also called relay), managed by volunteers, which allow anonymous outbound traffic and the creation of anonymous hidden services. Bridge relays are Tor relays that aren't listed in the main Tor directory. They are common referred when a filtering of connection is made by Internet Services Providers (ISP) to all the known Tor relays. It is important to specify that to directly access to a bridge it is necessary to know its address.

The Tor Metrics Portal provides in the Network many information regarding the network composition, in particular with the available statistics it is possible to analyze:

- Average daily number of relays and bridges in the network
- Average daily number of relays by country
- Relays with Exit, Fast, Guard, and Stable flags
- Relays by version
- Relays by platform
- Total relay bandwidth in the network
- Relay bandwidth by Exit and/or Guard flags
- Number of bytes spent on answering directory requests

The portal provides also statistics on the number of users that access to the TOR network via bridges to avoid monitoring systems put in place by government for surveillance purpose. The data could give an indication of the response of local government to the dissident communications.

The following graphs display an estimate of Tor users via bridges based on the unique IP addresses as seen by a few hundred bridges.

Figure 67 - Bridge users from all countries

Users accessing to the network

The Portal collects about the Tor network producing graphical representation regarding the analyses performed, for example it could be interesting to monitor a critical area and the access of population to the TOR network. In days for example in Syria a dictatorial regime is suppressing with military attacks the opponents to the government, in the same time it is using technological applications to avoid that population could transmit information regarding the suppression out of the country. The cyber experts of president Bashar al-Asad have also used several types of RAT (Remote Administration Tool) to prosecute dissidents. Let's analyze the number of directly connected users from the region in the last months.

The Deep Dark Web – the hidden web

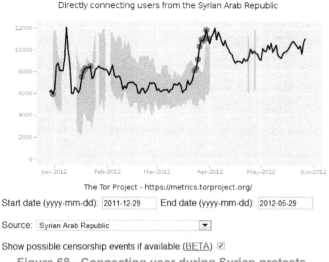

Directly connecting users from the Syrian Arab Republic

The Tor Project - https://metrics.torproject.org/

Start date (yyyy-mm-dd): 2011-12-29   End date (yyyy-mm-dd): 2012-05-29

Source: Syrian Arab Republic

Show possible censorship events if available (BETA) ☑

Figure 68 - Connecting user during Syrian protests

In the above picture the graphs related to the period between December 2011 and May 2012 that shows the progressive usage of the network in concomitance to political event. Very interesting a beta feature proposed by the web site that plots on the same graph with a different color possible censorship events.

Every time users are connected to a TOR network need to regular refresh their list of running relays. The users to save bandwidth of the directory authorities send their requests to one out of a few hundred directory mirrors, counting the number of the requests is possible to provide an estimate of the number of connected users. The graphs provide an estimate of recurring Tor users based on the number of sent requests received by few dozen directory mirrors.

Similar information could be used by intelligence services to monitor political evolution in specific areas.

The metric page also provides the list of Top-10 countries by directly connecting users and Top-10 countries by possible censorship events in beta version.

The Deep Dark Web – the hidden web

Top-10 countries by directly connecting users:

Start date (yyyy-mm-dd): 2011-12-29   End date (yyyy-mm-dd): 2012-05-29

[Update table]

Country	Mean daily users
United States	63529 (15.04 %)
Germany	40601 (9.61 %)
Iran	39968 (9.46 %)
Italy	35822 (8.48 %)
France	27735 (6.57 %)
Spain	24113 (5.71 %)
Russia	13001 (3.08 %)
Brazil	11889 (2.82 %)
United Kingdom	10056 (2.38 %)
Saudi Arabia	9205 (2.18 %)

Top-10 countries by possible censorship events (BETA):

Start date (yyyy-mm-dd): 2012-02-29   End date (yyyy-mm-dd): 2012-05-29

[Update table]

Country	Downturns	Upturns
China	14	17
Philippines	12	3
Ethiopia	10	6
Bangladesh	9	18
Lebanon	7	6
French Polynesia	7	2
Jamaica	6	6
Seychelles	6	0
United Republic of Tanzania	5	2
Kazakhstan	5	0

Figure 69 - Top-10 countries by directly connecting users

Packages requested from GetTor

The functionality GetTor allows users to fetch the Tor software via email, one of the proposed metrics on the portal shows the number of packages requested from GetTor daily. Crossing this information with statistics about the network usage, and in particular related to access mode through Tor bridges, it's possible verify the real motives behind the use of the network, the increasing of accessing users and the number of bridges it is fair to conclude that the intended audience is confronted with some form of censorship.

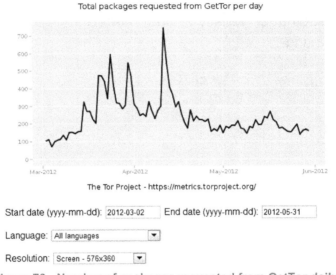

Figure 70 - Number of packages requested from GetTor daily.

Collection of active and passive performance measurements of the Tor network

The portal contains a set of graphs related the performance of the Tor network such as:

- the average (median) time to request files of three different sizes over Tor network

- fraction of timeouts and failures of downloading files over Tor as experienced by users. Following the definition for TOR Timeout and TOR Failure

  > *A **timeout*** occurs when a 50 KiB (1 MiB, 5 MiB) download does not complete within 4:55 minutes (29:55 minutes, 59:55 minutes).
  > *A **failure*** occurs when the download completes, but the response is smaller than 50 KiB (1 MiB, 5 MiB).

- fraction of connections that is used uni- or bi-directionally. Each connection is classified as "Mostly reading" or "Mostly writing," and "Both reading and writing."

Case Study – Ethiopia Introduces Deep Packet Inspection

The Ethiopian Telecommunication Corporation, unique telecommunication service provider of the country, has

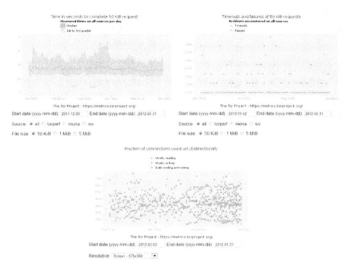

deployed for testing purpose a Deep Packet Inspection (DPI) of all Internet traffic.

Figure 71 - Performance Indicators

Let's try together to use monitoring systems. Let's set a time interval from the beginning of the year to date.

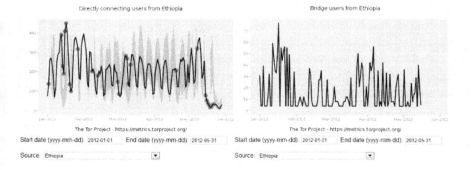

Analyzing the above graphs it's simple to note that in the last week of May the Tor Network was not accessible from the country even with trying to use bridged access, evidence of the presence of filtering system for Deep Packet Inspection. Websites such
as https://gmail.com/, https://facebook.com/, https://twitter.com/, and even https://torproject.org/ continue to work. The graphs below show the effects of this deployment of censorship based on Deep Packet Inspection:
Technically the filtering is made interfering with the handshake between Tor clients and Bridge servers, blocking the "TLS server hello" messages from the TOR bridges in response to a "TLS client hello".

Other Tor Metrics available on Internet

Of course the statistics published on the TOR portal provide a complete and clear vision of the usage of the network on different dimensions of analysis such as time and location, however in internet are available also other interesting report on the network. One of the most interesting reports is available at http://torstatus.all.de/, it provides information

regarding the available routers and relater attributes giving the possibility to the user to customize the analysis.

The portal give:

Figure 72 - TOR Status metrics

and querying the overall data to compose detailed reports:

- Show Aggregate Network Statistic Summary
- Show Network Status Opinion Source
- Custom / Advanced Display Options
- Show Custom / Advanced Query Options
- Show Table Legend
- Show Application Server Details

The Deep Dark Web – the hidden web

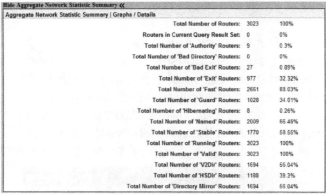

Figure 73 - Aggregate Statistics Summary

Another interesting source is the web site published by Atlas https://atlas.torproject.org/, a web application to discover Tor relays and bridges. It provides useful information on how relays are configured along with graphics about their past.

Figure 74 - Atlas Relay Info

The Future of ToR-.onion Network

The Future Of The Deep Dark Web

In today's world we want a little freedoms a little privacy online and more people will use encrypted methods to browse the web.- Julian Assange said it best-I paraphrase-, in society we as a online-person have an expectation to certain rights of privacy and just want 3 basic things:

1.) Freedom of Communication
2.) Freedom of Movement
3.) Freedom of Economics

In today's world our technology-culture encourages people to give away every detail of our life away. On Facebook, Twitter, LinkedIn we tell people all kind of personal information, everything you tell these website now belongs to them legally and they will do whatever they want with this data. They also want your shopping habits your reading habits and now they want to integrate it with other sites to extract more information. You don't think so, how many cookies do you have on your computer? -(I bet you don't have a clue) what were you doing at 5:30pm last Tuesday? Google knows, Facebook knows, Twitter knows, they all know. They all know your friends and your enemies.

Today's we are tied to cyberspace with almost every aspect of our lives – Social – Economy – Culture – Political – Ethics – Money – Wants' – Desires – Greed – So we want a Freedom of Communication, we want a secure -Tor anonymized type networks for some of our personal questions.

The Deep Dark Web – the hidden web

As more people use encrypted methods to browse the Web, it will become trickier for law enforcement agencies to intercept private communications in real-time, causing them to focus instead on tapping data that is stored in the cloud, according to the draft of an academic paper by a former privacy advisor to the Clinton Administration.

So this means that the legal beagles want to scare you more and more, we were just reading a post where someone said I don't like to cruise the dark web because I'm afraid of Identity Theft. In Tor-.onion network your secure with your identity, but if you log in to Facebook and start to give away your information well you just defeated what a Tor-style network does for you your anonymity is now gone.
Some segment of cyber-world will never need secure communication but we must ask what are our human values online? Are we ready to let everyone know the truth about oneself. The technology for anonymized network is here to stay and it's not good or bad, but it's powerful and a bit complicated. *The watchers of the Watch need to keep our eyes open for this one.*

References:

Tor Hidden Services by *administrator/MyHiddenBlog* –
Twitter Underground, Image Message Board – Pintrest –
Directory of some hidden services bookmark directory wiki –
Secure FTP – Search Engines….
Credits – one of the founder of the onion– Administrator –
Myhiddenblog@tormail.org
Index of all his sites. –

http://jm6miyk4tog63kqs.onion/TorStatusNet – **Twitter**

Undergroundhttp://lotjbov3gzzf23hc.onion/

TorStatusNet – lotjbov3gzzf23hc.onion is a **microblogging service**. Users post short (**1024 character**) notices which are broadcast to their friends and fans using the Web, RSS, or instant messages.
Hidden **Image Site Message Board** -

http://wyxwerboi3awzy23.onion/I2P link My Hidden Blog –

Directory of

OnionLandhttp://utup22qsb6ebeejs.onion/Freenet mirror

USK key I2P link

Onion**Bookmark** – Submit Onion

Sitehttp://x7yxqg5v4j6yzhti.onion/

Secure FTP -http://ldwvpjcrw5mmekvg.onion/

The Abyss – **Search Engine** http://nstmo7lvh4l32epo.onion/
Contact information: You can contact me through

tormailmyhiddenblog@tormail.org
use this hidden service to create
Tormail account.
http://jhiwjjlqpyawmpjx.onion

The Cleaned Hidden Wiki

http://3suaolltfj2xjksb.onion/hiddenwiki/index.php/Main_Page

Hidden services – HTTP/HTTPS

Volunteers last verified that all services in this section were up, or marked as DOWN, on: 2012-01-24

Introduction Points

OnionLand link indexes and search engines.

Hidden Wikis

Index pages in Wiki-based format.

HackBloc's Hidden Wiki Mirror – An editable up-to-date Hidden Wiki. Generally free from vandalism.

The Hidden Wiki – The original Hidden Wiki, owned by ion. Created January 2009. Went down for a while but it's back up now. A bit outdated.

Hidden Wiki Mirror – An old Hidden Wiki mirror. Outdated.

Other indexes

Other places/directories you may be able to find links.

OnionBookmark – Keep bookmarks private or share with public.

TORDIR – Categorized link list of Tor, user submitted. Also a PM service. (Provider: RA)

Sites Deep Web – A small list of onion links. (Host: FH)

Core.onion – Simple onion bootstrapping. (Provider: JA)

Search engines

Google for Tor. Search for links.

TORCH – Tor Search Engine. Claims to index around 1.1 Million pages.

Deepsearch – Another search engine.

Torgle – Torgle revived. Based on OnionWare's server. Web crawler.

The Abyss – Administrator's search engine. Supports submitted links.

Ahmia.fi – Clearnet search engine for Tor Hidden Services (allows you to add new sites to its database).

DuckDuckGo, clearnet – Clearnet metasearch engine with heavy filtering. Not like the aforementioned search engines to look up Hidden Services. Just searches the clearnet.

Other general stuff to see

Starting places.

Tor Web Design Guidelines – Suggestions to start making your own Hidden Service.

InspecTor – List of bad Tor nodes with ExcludeNodes generator for torrc. (Host: FH)

TorJump – A one-click wrapper to make Tor more accessible to non tech-savvies. (Host: FH)

Welcome, We've been expecting you! – Links to basic encryption guides.

Gateway – Tor ?? l2p web proxy.

Marketplace

See also: Marketplace Reviews – Reviews of the marketplace experience (ALL reviews go in this article, NOT in the listings below).See also: The separate Drugs and Erotica sections for those specific services. Remember that "feedback" can be faked in the Marketplace Reviews. Try to use escrow as much as possible to ensure you won't be scammed.

Financial Services

Currencies, banks, money markets, clearing houses, exchangers.

Anonymous Internet Banking Anonymous Debit Cards with EU bank account and VCCs by A HackBB trusted vendor

The Bitcoin Laundry Service- Bitcoin Laundry service.

InstaCard – Sell your bitCoins for a virtual VISA credit card, in $25, $50, or $100 denominations. $5 fee.

Paypal4free – Hacked PayPal accounts for cheap, with balances

PayPal Store – Purchase clean, verified USA PayPal accounts with Bitcoin. (Host: FH)

Bitcoin Fog – Laundry service.

anonXchange – Ecurrency exchanger, exchange LR, Bitcoin, PSC, Ukash, Pecunix, Cash. Also doing Bitcoin washing.

Acrimonious – A BitCoin escrow checkout. Free if there are no disputes. Works with tor2web. (UNABLE TO REGISTER)

Bitcoin2CC, clearnet – Converts your Bitcoins into a virtual VISA credit card instantly.

The Deep Dark Web – the hidden web

The Bitcoin Washing Machine – Can launder large amounts
of coins without same-coin contamination. (Host: FH)
Little BTC Ebook – The new way of selling and buying
Bitcoin is through Second Life, more information here.
Commercial Services
Mystery File a Day – Want to see something cool?
Brand New Microsoft Products – Brand new Microsoft
Hardware/Software up to 80% off Retail price. Start your
own eBay/Amazon Business.
Killer for Hire (Now Called C'thulhu) – Permanent Solutions
to Common Problems! (Cash/BitCoin/LR accepted)
Credit cards for all CCs from EU/US – Bitcoin. (WARNING:
http://xkhu7alqhs4ig3fu.onion/ is a Fake-Site!)
Megaupload.com Accounts for BTC – sells megaupload.com
accounts in exchange for bitCoins.
Quick Kill – Remove That Problem From Your Life.
(LR/Bitcoin)
Stolen Mac Store – We have many products, contact at
apple@tormail.net
Skimmers for SALE and RENT – No more fake CC IDs,
make your own!!
BitJack21, [clearnet - Bitcoin Blackjack.
Tor Poker - Tor Poker, gamble Bitcoins playing 5 card draw.
Two Glock 22 for sale Two Glock 22 for sale.
Help Guy - Work in your interests, business partner, friend or
whatever else.
EU Weapons - Europe Weapons and Ammunition (Pecunix,
Bitcoin). (Host: FH)
KordTusten Weapons and Firearms - Various guns for sale
with pictures.(Fake board)
All Purpose Identities - Get your Fake ID in the form of US
and Canada Drivers Licenses, passports and many more
Buttery Bootlegging - Get expensive items from major stores
for a fraction of the price! (Host: FH)
Stat ID's - Selling fake ID's.
Gun Guys Den (Sell's Firearms to Canada and US)
Red Dog Gaming - The Biggest and Best Casino on Tor:
Baccarat, BlackJack, Keno, Let It Ride, Three Card Poker,
Sports Book, Deposit Bonuses! Play Now!

Terminal Velocity United States Identification Store.

Patricks Mail Forward Mail forwarding service. DOWN 2012-01-27

PPSEE - The PayPal-Shop extreme Experience! (Bitcoin) FH (under construction)

FreshTec - SCAM! A bounty is being put on you unless our money is returned by the fifth, you've been warned.

Tor University (#1st) -

BitCoin - Like EBay. We increase the gross national product. (Host: FH)

Fixed Match Service - Fixed Match Service. Lets you buy into fixed sporting events. (Host: FH)

Cheap SWATTING Service - Calls in raids as pranks. (Host: FH)

Data-Bay - Buy and sell files using digital currency.

Tor University (#2nd) - Research and Writing services for the college student. (Host: FH)

Pirax Web DDoS - Take out your enemies in seconds. (Host: FH)

Onion-ID Get your 2nd identity from Onion-ID, real passports and professional id card + drivers license replicas.

Hacking Services - Hacks IM and Social Nets, does DDoS, sells bank/credit/PayPal accounts. Se Habla Espanol. (Host: FH)

Slash'EM online - Super Lots'A Stuff Hack-Extended Magic tournament server (Bitcoin).

Rent-a-Hacker - Professional hacker for hire, DDOS, hacking, ruining people, espionage etc.

Contract Killer - Kill your problem (snitch, paparazzo, rich husband, cop, judge, competition, etc). (Host: FH)

BacKopy - Sells game, software and movie discs (Bitcoin).

Flip the coin, get the money! - A simple coin tossing game with 50-50 chance.

Assassination Market - A market following the "Assassination Politics"

Underground Market Board - Underground Market Board is intended to be used as a market.

FancyPower Macbooks - "Acquired" Macbook Pros and Airs for sale. (404 Not Found) - Broken 2012-01-29

Underground Market Board
Downloaditforyou - File Download Service. We download
files, burn them to DVD's and send them to you in the mail.
Hosting / Web / File / Image
The Onion Cloud - Tor/ownCloud based cloud. Login/Pass:
public/public. (Host: FH)
Megaupload.com Accounts for BTC - sells megaupload.com
accounts in exchange for bitCoins
TOR host - Host your site anonymously in deep web for free.
- DOWN 2011-12-24
bittit, clearnet - Host and sell your original pictures for
Bitcoins.
Mystery File a Day - Want to see something cool?
Blolylo - Simple file uploads. Won't accept plain text files. 2
MiB upload limit. (Host: FH) (Blank page) - Broken 2011-06-
09
CircleServices - Mixie's place. Provides: Circle-Talk, TorPM,
ImgZapr, SnapBBS, qPasteBin, AnonyShares, Circle-IRC.
(Provider: CS)
Anonyshares - File upload up to 10MB. (Provider: CS)
qPasteBin - A pastebin. (Provider: CS)
5am - File dump and Image Board. 5MB Limit. DOWN 2012-
01-05
Potaoto - Image hosting. Generates large thumbnails.
DOWN 2012-01-05
Onion Fileshare - 2GB Upload file size limit. Upload any files
you want.
ES Simple Uploader - Upload images, docs and other files. 2
MiB upload limit. (Host: FH)
IMGuru (More info) - Fast GIF/JPEG host. No images
removed. If you get the error Invalid File, retry the upload.
(Host: FH)
TorIB - Create and run your own imageboard. (Host: FH)
(Neglected status note) - Broken 2010-06-16
SquareBoard - Upload and share high quality images.
(Moderated)
sTORage - Upload files. Has WebDAV support.
Onion Image Uploader - Image Hosting. 2 MiB upload limit.
Generates medium thumbnails. (Host: FH)

Freedom Hosting (More info) - Hosting Service with PHP/MySQL. As of 2011-06-04, it hosts about 50% of the live OnionWeb by onion. UPDATE 2011-06-05, probably owns a lot more than that now. Invite-only.

PasteOnion - Paste and share text, sources, whatever. You can make your paste public or set a password. (Host: FH)

QicPic - Upload any type of file. Caches and compresses uploaded files to decrease loading time. (Host: FH)

Blogs / Essays

Nekro's Onion Shanty #Revived# - A personal page by Nekro.

My Hidden Blog - Security politics, security, tor, tools, personal.

The Most Dangerous Man in Cyberspace - Scans of a Rolling Stone article about Jacob Appelbaum (ioerror).

RespiraTOR - If something is infuriating you, it's better to get it off your chest (Host: FH) (not updated since November 2011)

Americans for Disparity - Exploring disparity.

Tor and blosxom - A Tor hidden service running on the blosxom blogging platform.

Coding Horror - Programming and human factors. DOWN 2012-01-24

The Croat's Blog - It's all about the Intel and knowledge! Whistle blowing FTW! (Host: FH) (Absolutely no content. But up.)

10 Step Guide to Bail Jumping - More about Jumping bail and fleeing the country (Host: FH)

Gionn.net, clearnet - Technology blog and news aggregator.

My Hidden Blog - Security politics, security, tor, tools, personal.

Tornado - Forum, blogs, polls, registered or anon posting. User List. (Host: FH)

Radio Free KENK - Music, media, anarchy. By: qfkenk. (Host: FH) (404 Not Found) - Broken 2012-01-16

Shew's Blog #1st - Redirects Meta to: Shew's Blog #2nd. (Host: FH) - Redir 2011-08-01

Shew's Blog #2nd - Blog and Shewstring, an anonymized FreeBSD distro, open commenting. (Host: FH) (not updated since 2011-09-04)

Cone's lair #2nd - Yeesha. Back with Cone's journal and some other stuff.

True Anonymous Confessions - A confession service based on a bash clone. (Host: FH)

Beat Charges - Beat Criminal Charges, pass your sex offender polygraph, flee the country. beatcharges@tormail.net for special consultation / Bitcoin payment options.

How to Get Away with Insider Trading - You always wondered why these guys were getting caught, now pull it off and make millions.

Beat the Sex Offender Polygraph & Abel Assessment - Sex Offender? Here's how to stay out and prevent re-convictions or get a better plea offer.

TORus.net - A micro-blogging service based on the Free Software StatusNet tool. DOWN 2012-01-16

Beneath VT - Information on the steam tunnels at Virginia Tech.

Keep Bitcoin Real, flickr, imgur - Fuck the day traders, take Bitcoin back to its roots. (Host: FH)

The Human Experiment - Human medical experiments. We go, where few dare. (Host: FH)(Direct FH URL). (Host: FH)

- Steal This Wiki mirror - Steal this wiki mirror, no editing, hosted at NoReason.

Forums / Boards / Chans

SnapBBS

A relatively simplistic messaging board owned by Mixie. Various discussion boards. There's lots of these, but here are a couple.

TheHiddenHand - SnapBBS, TheHiddenHand collective communication based on conspiracy, philosophy and uncensored information

Circle-Talk - A board on the front page of CircleService. (Provider: CS)

SnapBBS - The SnapBBS service. A temporary dump of the public board index is here. (Provider: CS)

Onion Site Reviews - A site started 2011/11/19 made for the reviews of onion sites. (Host: CS)

TorTSE - A continuation of the infamous TOTSE forum which has existed since the late 80s covering almost every topic. (Host: CS)

TOR Free For All - Un-moderated area for political and other topics. Anything goes. Private board. (Host: CS)

Democrat Watch - Right-wing board dedicated to criticizing Democrats (registration required). (Host: CS)

The Intel Exchange - Know or need to know something? Ask and share at this underground intelligence gathering network. (Host: CS)

LE+TOR Interchat - Law enforcement and Tor users can interact and share their opinions as humans. (Host: CS)

TOR Answers - Like Yahoo answers, but with a Tor twist. (Host: CS)

Paranomal Aliens n' Shit - Discussion of the Paranormal, Aliens and Shit. (Host: CS)

Cafe at the End of the Internet - Feeling off-topic? Tech-oriented chill zone/meeting grounds for general talk. (Host: CS)

Esoteric and Occult - Dedicated to all forms of occultism. (Host: CS)

Crime Network - A place to network and get better at your craft. (Host: CS)

Demosthenes' Board - Demosthenes' Board. (Host: CS)

SnapBBS public board - The public SnapBBS board. (Provider: CS)

What is your current Bitch? Post your current gripe and/or bitch! Blow some steam off and you will feel better.

Alternative Energy Forum - Talk about energy projects with other people.

Other forums

Other forum types. Usually phpBB.

Circle-Talk - A board on the front page of CircleService. (Provider: CS)

Torduckin0 #1st - Citadel BBS with chat and IM to support Torduckin. (Provider: JF)

Onionforum 2.0 - A restart of the popular Onionforum. No login required. (Host: FH)

OnionTalk - 2ch-inspired messaging board. No registration required! DOWN 2012-01-22

Talk.Masked, clearnet contact form - Talks and Notes. 2nd generation. Famous messaging board. (Provider: JA)

Torduckin0 #2nd - Citadel BBS with chat and IM to support Torduckin. (Provider: JF)

Anonymous BBS, gopher interface, telnet interface - Another variation of the talk's style of board.

OnionMe - Forum for personal ads. All ages' welcome.

Torduckin0 #3rd - Citadel BBS with chat and IM to support Torduckin. (Provider: JF)

Torduckin0 #4th - Citadel BBS with chat and IM to support Torduckin. (Provider: JF)

Leaf's underground horticulture - Minimalist, multipurpose text boards. No login required. (Host: FH)

EpicIB - Private IB/Chan hosting by Onionymous. Boards: /tib (A TinyIB) (needs to be configured) - Broken 2012-01-23

Torsquare - Anonymous board, shares posts and discussions with Torbook's public square.

HackBB - Forums for hacking, carding, cracking, programming, anti-forensics, and other tech topics. Also a marketplace with escrow. Should be H/P/A/W/V/C but it can go under here as well.

Freeside - WHY WAIT? Leave the crazy at the door.

RedditTor - Anonymous Reddit. Broken until further notice.

Imageboards

Non-CP or generally safe imageboards on Tor.

Torchan - /b/, /i/, programming, revolution, tons of other boards

Anonchan - Boards: /b/ - Random, /a/ - Anime/Manga/NSFW.

Hidden Image Site - HIS

TriChan - Revived, now only has /p/ Pokemon, /mlp/ My Little Pony, and /b/ Random

Lukochan - A Russian/English text discussion board in imageboard style.

Deaths (R.I.P):

RundaChan - Share ideas and ask or answer questions
Bobby's board Channel with currently only 2 boards but
growing - about 75% LOL 0% uptime
Forums Scripts Besides SnapBBS
PunBB 1.3.6 Forum script - During installation, you need not
give your email address to create your forum! When
registering you do not need feeding your e-mail! You can
register without e-mail. The script does not register in the
forum database your IP! nor the Administrator / Moderator
cannot see your IP address gives you a much safer use of
the forum because your IP is not logged anywhere in the
database! Two mirrors download.
If anyone knows of anything else that provides this, send an
e-mail.
Email / Messaging
See also: The compendium of clearnet Email providers.
Startbook - online management of your bookmarks/favorites
TorPM - Tor Private Messaging. (Provider: CS)
SimplePM - A PM service by CWKU. No registration needed.
(Host: FH)
GPF AnonymousWebservices, clearnet - Proxies for I2P,
mail, news, tor, web. By: GermanPrivacyFoundation
Anonymoose Chat - An HTML-only chatroom. (Host: FH)
(doesn't work) - Broken 2012-01-23
GPF PrivacyBox, clearnet - Private messaging service.
Proxies for I2P, tor, web. By: GermanPrivacyFoundation
Tor Mail - Webmail/SMTP/IMAP/POP3. Can send/receive
mail from outside Tor with a you@tormail.net address.
Remailer Reliability Stats, clearnet, clearnet -
Mixmaster/Cypherpunk remailer stats.
mul.tiver.se, clearnet - Censorship-free distributed social
network hosted by the Chinese Pirate Party DOWN 2012-01-
05
Newzbin, clearnet - Crowdsourced Usenet index based in
the UK
ChatRoom - BlaB! Lite AJAX based chat system, use any
browser. No registration. (Host: FH)
EFG Chat - HTTP refresh chatrooms. (Host: FH)
Torbook - A way to make friends in onionland.

ELIZA - Free psychotherapy!
n0id - n0id's crypto identity and contact page.
Narcan's GPG key - Narcan's GPG key. (Host: FH)
TorStatusNet - Twitter clone on tor.
Political Advocacy
Heidenwut - Politics, Occultism, Spy vs. Spy, Revolution!!
clearnet
BuggedPlanet.Info - Information on Telecommunication
Interception Companies & Installations
PURE EUROPE - Cleanse Europe of the dirt! (Host: FH)
Keep Internet Open! - Small unofficial AnonOps site,
currently instructing how to DDoS MasterCard and other
WikiLeaks opponents.
A website - Free speech advocacy. (About 50% uptime.)
paraZite #2nd, clearnet 301 redirector - paraZite: Illicit
activities advocacy and censored information archive.
Neutering NOT Org, clearnet - Why Non-Human Beings
Should NOT Be Castrated. Has WolfHowl.Org mirror. (Host:
FH)
House of Anonymous - Satirical manifesto regarding
anonymous. (Host: FH)
paraZite #1st, clearnet 301 redirector - paraZite: Illicit
activities advocacy and censored information archive.
FREEFOR - USA-based FREEdom FORces developing a
turnkey distributed Temporary Autonomous Zone. FAQ
The Movement of Torism - New activist group organized in
OnionSpace. (Host: FH)
Wake up Europe! - This is a call to arms!
Revolution Bunker - h3x's blog on censorship, hacking,
privacy, crypto, capitalism, war, corruption, etc. (Host: FH)
(not updated since August 2011)
LoM's Revolutionary Codex - Revolution/Subversive texts,
forum soon, blog. (Host: FH) (not updated since November
2010)
Heidenwut - Politics, Occultism, Spy vs Spy, Revolution!!
(Host: FH)
Whistleblowing
WikiLeaks

See also: WikiLeaks Official Site and Official Submission Onion (temporarily closed).

A Cat's Mirror of Wikileaks Cablegate site, clearnet - Includes cables currently redacted or offline.

WikiLeaks mirror #B - updates follow wikileaks.ch with up to 3 days delay.

WikiLeaks mirror #A - WikiLeaks last push update to this mirror occurred 2011-03-06.

Operation AntiSec

Operation Satiagraha, clearnet - Evidence exposing high-level corruption in Brazil.DOWN 2012-01-21

Fuck FBI Friday IV: Vanguard Defense Industries - Private documents from a military contractor. DOWN 2012-01-23

Texas Takedown Thursday: Chinga La Migra IV - AntiSec messes with Texas, attacks dozens of police systems and chief emails.

Fuck FBI Friday: IACIS Cybercrime Investigator Communications - email dump including IACIS internal email list archives

Other

Freedom of Information Network - Leak document safely. Anonymous registration required. No logs. Get a spot in our bunker. DOWN 2012-01-10

A website - Advocates free speech and accepts new leaks. DOWN 2012-01-10

HBGary Federal Attachment Dump - The HBGary email archive leaked by Anonymous. (Host: FH)

Zyprexa Kills, mirror - The Zyprexa Memos. Internal documents that Eli Lilly tried to censor. (HTML contains a syntax error) - Broken 2012-01-24

Taz.de, clearnet - Mockup of another leak project, known as OpenLeaks. DO NOT USE FOR SERIOUS LEAKS.

H/P/A/W/V/C

Hack, Phreak, Anarchy (internet), Warez, Virus, Crack.

DOXBIN - DOX go here. A pastebin for personally identifiable information.

HackBB - Forums for hacking, carding, cracking, programming, anti-forensics, and other tech topics. Includes a marketplace with escrow.

VIAGRA - Read-only site with archives of files/texts related to hacking/security. DOWN 2012-01-09
Carders Forums - Ministry of Fraudulently Affairs.
hashparty - Password hash cracking site.
Kaspersky Key Share - Get KAV and KIS keys here. DB ERROR (Provider: RA)
OnionWarez - Warez forum
Polyfront #2nd (mirror) - Tradecraft and security tutorials
OpenSource Intelligence - LEA ops capability docs with an emphasis on cyber crime DOWN 2012-01-17
OnionUserX Censor Page - Seriously, the fuck? Anyone mind reposting the original links?
The KMs Bird (WhiteHex) - School hacker. (Host: FH)
DeepSec, clearnet - An annual European two-day in-depth conference on computer, network, and application security.
BRAMA - Linux/Wireless/Mobile tech consortium in Poland.
TM Comm - For a Chaotic Tomorrow. (Host: FH)
The KMs Bird (GreenBin) - School hacker. (Host: FH)
Shell In A Box - Shell In A Box.
Requiem - Software for removing iTunes DRM
keys open doors - Mirror of geohot's PS3 hacking tools (censored on the clearnet by a Sony lawsuit)
Speakeasy #2nd - Paper describing a highly-secured forum system (current version). (Host: FH)
Crackwar - Pirates are the good guys! (Host: FH)
Cycekkk - A browser exploit page using 302 mailto method. Tries to send bad words/links to Mr. Brejza. (Host: FH)
Weird and Wonderful Old Stuff - A collection of old DOS and Windows software. (Host: FH)
PayPal Store (no contact info) - Broken 2012-01-29
New Diceware Lists - Randomization for file names. Multiple lists, more to come. (Host: FH)
Speakeasy #1st - Paper describing a highly-secured forum system (old flawed version). (Host: FH)
Onion Desktop - eyeOS web desktop. (Host: FH)
Dear PayPal, (clearnet) - AntiSec's message.
thE LisT oF SQL data bases! - MySQL credentials archive. Hosted on this page.

bugmenot@tor - A user supplied database of account credentials for various websites.

Audio - Music / Streams

Lossless Audio Files - Mostly WavPack, some FLAC, Ape, ogg, etc. Has index generating links.

Video - Movies / TV

FileshareZ Filesharing forum, movies, music and tv-shows. (Host: FH)

Movies, Music, TV & Ebooks user: webuser password: L0L******

Books

See also: Category:Novel - List of books on this wiki.

The Tor Library - 47 GB. pdf, chm, djvu. Design by Russebertene

Example rendezvous points page - Thomas Paine's *Common Sense* and *The Federalist papers*

Destination Unknown - Small selection. Searchlores, Cryptonomicon, Thelema...

LiberaTor - Making weapons, military training, and related subjects. (Host: FH)

Free Bibliotheca Alexandrina - English, Spanish and German book fileserver and wiki. Mostly sf/fantasy. (Host: FH)

The Laughing Nihilist - Drugs + writing. (Host: FH)

Mister's Library - Mostly philosophical. (Host: FH) (403 Forbidden) - Broken 2012-01-23

Mister - Collection of writings, art, selected texts and deeply personal views on philosophy of existence. (Host: FH)

ParaZite - Collection of forbidden files and how-to's (pdf, txt, etc.).

Drugs

Noncommercial (D)

These sites have only drug-related information/talk. No sales or venues.

Silk Road Forums - Silk Road Forums

Be Here Now - The North American Laughing Buddha (Folk medical advice from a pothead). (Host: FH)

TorDrugResource - Drug Chemistry and Pharmacology including limited Rhodium/Hive/Synthetikal mirrors. (Host: FH)

Serenity Files - Community-maintained library on growing elicit substances.
Commercial (D)
See also: Marketplace Reviews and Onion Reviews - Reviews of the marketplace experience (ALL reviews go in these articles, NOT in the listings below).
oxiD Shop - Marijuana, Cocaine (Bitcoin)
Silk Road - Marketplace with escrow (Bitcoin)
Pot2Peer - Marijuana and cannabis products delivered safely and discreetly to your door. Always anonymous. (Bitcoin)
Paradoxum - Cannabis, MDMA, LSD, Mushrooms, Coke, DMT (BTC, Dwolla, Pecunix, LR, Paxum)
DrugSpace - Dispensary Grade Sour Diesel Marijuana and Cambodian strain Psilocybin Mushrooms. Get the URL from the Onion Reviews, people keep changing it here
Trees by Mail Beta - Cannabis from Northern California (Bitcoin)
and - Yummy edibles and other cannabis related stuff. Nothing but the best. (PayPal and Bitcoin)
Erotica
Adult
Noncommercial (E)
(Y)APE - Yet Another Porn Exchange.
LustAdultery - Hardcore hot truth ladies and lust
Bug Tales - Site rip of Bugtales.net from the Internet Archive. Homosexual bug chasing stories. (Host: FH)
Porn-Free - Free porn advice
Hard p0rn - forum - The harder the better
Penis Panic! - Dedicated to genital mutilation. The discussion board. (Host: CS)
Penis Panic! - Dedicated to genital mutilation. The pictures and videos. (Host: FH)
Commercial (E)
See also: Marketplace Reviews - Reviews of the marketplace experience (ALL reviews go in this article, NOT in the listings below).
Fap BTC - Buy accounts for porn sites.

bittit NSFW, clearnet - Buy or sell original NSFW pictures for Bitcoins.

CambodiaSite - rent-a-friend for sex-tourists in Cambodia

XXX Passes and stuff - Passes to various sites (BTC). (Host: FH)

Passwords and other things - Passwords to most XXX sites and other things (Bitcoin). (Host: FH)

XXX Passwords - Popular XXX site passwords (Bitcoin). (Host: FH)

XXX Passwords - Popular XXX site passwords (Bitcoin). (Host: FH) (Has no contact info) - Broken 2011-07-06

Tor Sex Workers Review Board - For escorts, exotics, massage, etc. (Host: FH)

Paraphilias

VOR-COM Archive - Archive of the VOR-COM. Contains vore!

Watersports and piss - Watersports and piss. (Host: CS)

The Secret Story Archive #1st - Big cat zoophile stories, artwork, links and forum.

The Secret Story Archive #2nd - Mirror of #1st.9

Anessadu's file dump, tor2web redirect - Furry Blender images.

Uncategorized

Services that defy categorization, or that have not yet been sorted.

Kenny - You killed Kenny! You're a bastard! DOWN

Carson - Nature Boy poem. Previously The Ultimate Guide for Anonymous and Secure Internet Usage v1.0.1.

The LG enV2 - Very basic information and photo gallery about a wireless digital messaging phone. (Host: FH)

Questions and Answers - A little truth game. Ask questions and give answers anonymously. Answers also support image uploading.

noreason - Info and pdf files on weapons, locks, survival, poisons, protesters, how to kill. Hidden Wiki, TorDir, Steal this wiki, Telecomix Crypto Munitions Bureau mirrors. Guro, dofantasy / Fansadox Collection. DOWN D:

The Outlaw Project - "Free for all" - links to various files and known .onion sites. Onion address hosted an FTP service.

Fenergy file-server - File collection that includes books and other resources energy related.
Non-English
Czech / ?eština
http://n4k727nqnwkvb4g6.onion/d/ - Free speech advocates, news and articles about Big Brother, 1984 etc. DOWN 2012-01-24
PirateLeaks.cz #2nd, clearnet - ?eská obdoba WikiLeaks / Czech website based on Wikileaks.
Danish / Dansk
DanishChan - Scandinavian focused imageboard. Boards include drugs and IT security as well as a Random board. Fast and clean layout, little downtime.
drugs.dk - Danish Drug Trade. (Host: CS)
Dutch / Nederland's
Voetbalfan - Voetbalfan. (Host: FH)
Estonian / Eesti
Vileveeb - Anonüümsete raportite esitamine. DOWN 2012-01-24
Finnish / Suomi
Sipulilauta - A chan. (Direct FH URL) (Host: FH)
Sipulilauta - A chan. (Host: FH)
Thorlauta - Successor to Torlauta.
Blue Quarters - Advice regarding to BitCoins, Silk Road Online, ordering anonymously, staying anonymous in deepweb etc.
Blue Quarters Forum - Discussion forum.
TorBook - Discussion forum, marketplace. DOWN 2012-01-24
Suojeluskunta - White Power Forum
French / Français
Noel Board - A French board.
Je suis Kalila - Weird website.
Forum Hacking-Security
German / Deutsch
Das ist DEUTSCHLAND hier - discussion forum with no specific topic. (Host: FH)

TAZ Archiv - A daily updated archive of the TAZ (German newspaper) starting from 2009-05 maybe with some days missing

Warez Forum - Forum for warez and uncensored talk. (Host: FH)

Archiv der Aktiven-Mailingliste der Piratenpartei Deutschland,

beaglesnoop - Website and blog. (Host: FH)

Zwiebelpad v1.1 - An EtherPad. (Provider: TS) DOWN 2012-01-24

Pyrowiki - Pyrotechnics and drug wiki. (Host: FH)

Dissoziation - Wiki about dissociation, multiplicity, trauma, etc. (site is blank) - Broken 2012-01-24

Geheimkanal - Imageboard. (Partially 18+). (Host: FH)

Safety101 - Computer safety board. Some English. (Host: FH)

Hebrew / ?????

Samim.onion - Selling and shipping of drugs and medicine in Israel (Bitcoin). (Host: FH)

Italian / Italiano

Cipolla (se offline andate qui) - Forum italiano: Mercatino, Hacking, Bitcoin, Droghe ...

Deepwiki ITA Eciclopedia libera italiana

TutankEmule, clearnet - Emule/ed2k link index DOWN 2012-01-24

Il blog di leandro

ITALY: Mercato nero

Japanese / ???

Tor Links - ?????????????????????????????????????

Vacatin City - ?????????????????????

201Q - 201Q 1

201Q - 201Q 2

201Q 2ch - 201Q 2ch type

room 201Q - Room 201Q

After Dark - we are all alone

rococo city #2nd - ??han?BBS. ??????????

????????? - ?????????????

Erotica Romance #2nd - ????? ????

Erotica Romance #1st - Erotica, Romance

Onion????? - Onion Channel, a system similar to 2channel.
Tor Land in Japan - Tor BBS. ??????????????Finally
Free????. (Host: FH)
Tor ??? - Tor????Finally Free??????. (Host: FH)
201Q Y - ??????. (Host: FH)
phpFreeChat - ???????????????????????
????????????????????????????? ?????????????. (Host:
FH)
???BBS? - ???????. (hentai image board) (Host: FH)
Korean / ???
?? - ??? ?? ??? (??????)
Polish / Polski
Torowisko - Forum Polskiej Spo?eczno?ci Tor. Nowe
ogólnotematyczne forum bez rejestracji i cenzury. Godny
Nast?pca Onionforum, ju? z ponad 8000 postami
(codziennie przybywaj? nowe!). (Host: FH)
Fundacja Panoptykon, clearnet - Strona fundacji
przeciwstawiaj?cej si? coraz powszechniejszej inwigilacji
oraz tendencjom nasilania nadzoru i kontroli nad
spo?ecze?stwem.
George Orwell "Rok 1984" - polskie t?umaczenie znanej
powie?ci
Polska Ukryta Wiki - PUW, wiki polskiej spo?eczno?ci Tor.
(Host: FH)
FAQ – Freely Answered Questions - Portal typu Q&A, gdzie
mo?esz zadawa? pytania zwi?zane z undergroundem (czyt.
pytania niewygodne). (Host: FH)
Strony porzucone, nieaktywne lub ?mieciowe:
Backup NWO - wybór najciekawszych stron i artyku?ów dot.
nowego porz?dku ?wiata i tematów pokrewnych. (Host: FH)
Ksi?ga Urantii - czyli kolejna, jedynie s?uszna prawda,
komu? tam objawiona. (Host: FH)
Krzysztof Brejza - ma?o zabawna imitacja strony jednego z
pos?ów PO. (Host: FH)
Polska Cebulka - blog i zbiór linków dot. polskich zasobów
sieci Tor. (Host: FH)
Polska ukryta strona w sieci Tor - przyk?adowa strona.
(Host: FH)

Torkazywarka i Forum Przekr?ty, praktycznie martwe forum, w za?o?eniu o przekr?tach, broni i hackingu. (Host: FH)
TorKnight - wielotematyczne forum wymagaj?ce rejestracji. (Host: FH)
56 Dog Days - Ramblings. (Host: FH)
Onioon Search - Polska wyszukiwarka stron .onion - ka?dy mo?e doda? swój stron? do katalogu wyszukiwarki. (Host: FH)
Portuguese / Portugues
Caravana Brasil
Russian / ???????
R2D2 - ????????? ?????, ??????? ???????????, ???????? ????????
Runion - ????????? ?????: Bitcoin, Tor, ????????? ?????
Runion Wiki - ??????? ?????? ? ????????? ? Runion ?? ???????
??????? - ??????? ??????? ?????. (Host: FH)
???? - ??????????? ???????? ???????? ????????????. (Host: FH)
??? - ????????? ???????????? ?????.
????????, clearnet - ?????? ???????? ????????????? ????????? ????????.
?????-?????? - ????? ??????? ?????? ? ???? ?? ??????? ?????. (Host: FH)
Russian Road - ??????? Silk Road(?????????, ??????, ?????????, ?????????)
Slovak / Slovenský
Detská pornografia: Je to len zámienka - Pre?o je boj proti detskej pornografii zámienkou pre nie?o iné. (Host: FH)
Spanish / Español
Abusos - Abusos judiciales en España.
Quema tu móvil!, clearnet - Interceptación de comunicaciones móviles. Cell phone eavesdropping techniques used by Intel agencies. DOWN 2012-01-24
HoneyNet, clearnet - Hacking ético, técnicas especiales de seguridad empleadas en los test de intrusión para evitar ser detectados. DOWN 2012-01-24
T0rtilla - Shoutox webchat. (Host: FH)
CebollaChan - CebollaChan, el tor-chan en Castellano.

T0rtilla - Shoutbox webchat. (Direct FH URL). (Host: FH)
Forocoches 2.0 - Torocoches - Forocoches 2.0 (Host: FH)
Swedish / Svenska
Moral.Nu, clearnet - Vad är moral? (Provider: RE)
KognitionsKyrkan, clearnet - Spiritual stuff. (Provider: RE)
ZG Projektet, clearnet - ZG Projektet. (Provider: RE)
Hidden Services - Other Protocols
Volunteers last verified that all services in this section were up, or marked as DOWN, on: 2011-06-08For configuration and service/uptime testing, all services in this section MUST list the active port in their address. Exception: HTTP on 80, HTTPS on 443.For help with configuration, see the TorifyHOWTO and End-to-end connectivity issues.
P2P FileSharing
Running P2P protocols within Tor requires OnionCat. Therefore, see the OnionCat section for those P2P services.IMPORTANT: It is possible to use Tor for P2P. However, if you do, the right thing must also be done by giving back the bandwidth used. Otherwise, if this is not done, Tor will be crushed taking everyone along with it.
The Pirate Bay - Download music, movies, games, software! The Pirate Bay - The galaxy's most resilient BitTorrent site - Official(?)
GNUnet files sharing - GNUnet URI index site with forum. (Host: FH)
Sea Kitten Palace - Torrent site and tracker for extreme content (real gore, animal torture, shockumentaries/mondo cinema, and Disney movies)
AshANitY - Anonymous sharing of Humanity, torrents. (Host: FH)
Chat centric services
Some people and their usual server hangouts may be found in the Contact Directory.
IRC
See also: IRC Anonymity Guide
AnoNet - Each server is on its own network and connects to a chat cloud

irc1.srn.ano, clearnet
elef7kcrczguvamt.onion:15783 - Direct access to the AnoNet
chat cloud. Use an IRC server to connect.
irc3.srn.ano
irc2.srn.ano, clearnet - Still connects to the old AnoNet chat
cloud; that will soon change.
irc4.srn.ano
irc.cananon.ano Web Chat Version join #AnoNet
OFTC IRC - OFTC IRC server
running on: (various).oftc.net, ports:: plaintext: 6667 ssl:
6697
Federation: OnionNet - IRC network comprised of:
Circle IRC - Circle IRC server. (Provider: CS)
FTW IRC - FTW IRC server.
Nissehult IRC - Nissehult IRC server.
Renko IRC - Renko IRC Server.
OpenSource, info - Drug chat
Dark Tunnel Irc2p gateway - Gateway to the Irc2p IRC
network on I2P.
running on: unknown, ports:: plaintext: 6668, ssl: none
Chi's Tunnel to Irc2p - New Gateway to the Irc2p IRC
network (old one was down)

freenode IRC - freenode IRC server
running on: (various).freenode.net, ports:: plaintext: 6667 ssl:
6697/7070
NeoturbineNET IRC - NeoturbineNET IRC server
running on: kropotkin.computersforpeace.net, ports::
plaintext: none ssl: 6697
FREEFOR - FREEdom FORces - see "Political Advocacy"
running on: unknown, ports:: plaintext: 6667 ssl: 9999
hackint - hackint is a communication network for the hacker
community.
running on: lechuck.darmstadt.ccc.de, ports:: plaintext: none
ssl: 6697
Agora Anonymous - Agorist IRC server
HeavyCrypto - HeavyCrypto IRC
running on: unknown, ports:: ssl: 6697
SILC

fxb4654tpptq255w.onion:706 - SILCroad, public server. [discuss/support]

XMPP (formerly Jabber)

xmpp:ch4an3siqc436soc.onion:5222 – public server. No SSL. Chatrooms. No S2S. – DOWN 2011-08-01

xmpp:okj7xc6j2szr2y75.onion:5222 –

xmpp:jabber.ccc.de:5222 as a hidden service

TorChat Addresses

Humans are listed in the above contact directory. Bots are listed below.

7oj5u53estwg2pvu.onion:11009 – TorChat InfoServ #2nd, by ACS.

gfxvz7ff3bzrtmu4.onion:11009 – TorChat InfoServ #1st, by ACS.

OnionCat Addresses

List of only the Tor-backed fd87:d87e:eb43::/48 address space, sorted by onion. There are instructions for using OnionCat, Gnutella, BitTorrent Client, and BitTorrent Tracker.

62bwjldt7fq2zgqa.onion:8060

fd87:d87e:eb43:f683:64ac:73f9:61ac:9a00 – ICMPv6 Echo Reply

a5ccbdkubbr2jlcp.onion:8060 – mail.onion.aio

fd87:d87e:eb43:0744:208d:5408:63a4:ac4f – ICMPv6 Echo Reply

ce2irrcozpei33e6.onion:8060 – bank-killah

fd87:d87e:eb43:1134:88c4:4ecb:c88d:ec9e – ICMPv6 Echo Reply

[fd87:d87e:eb43:1134:88c4:4ecb:c88d:ec9e]:8333 – Bitcoin Seed Node

taswebqlseworuhc.onion:8060 – TasWeb – DOWN 2011-09-08

fd87:d87e:eb43:9825:6206:0b91:2ce8:d0e2 – ICMPv6 Echo Reply

http://[fd87:d87e:eb43:9825:6206:0b91:2ce8:d0e2]/

gopher://[fd87:d87e:eb43:9825:6206:0b91:2ce8:d0e2]:70/

vso3r6cmjoomhhgg.onion:8060 – echelon

fd87:d87e:eb43:ac9d:b8f8:4c4b:9cc3:9cc6 – ICMPv6 Echo Reply

Bitcoin Seeding

Instructions

bitcoinbudtoeks7.onion:8333 – DOWN 2011-08-20

nlnsivjku4x4lu5n.onion:8333 – DOWN 2011-08-20

xqzfakpeuvrobvpj.onion:8333

z6ouhybzcv4zg7q3.onion:8333

Dead Hidden Services

Main article: List of dead hidden services

Do not simply remove services that appear to be offline from the above list! Services can go down temporarily, so we keep track of when they do and maintain a list of dead hidden services.

In addition to an onion simply being gone (Tor cannot resolve the onion), sites that display 404 (and use a known onion/URL based hosting service) are the only other things that are considered truly DOWN. Presumably the account is gone.

If a service has been down for a while, tag it with ' – DOWN YYYY-MM-DD' (your guess as to when it went down).

If a tagged service on the above list of live hidden services has come back up, remove the DOWN tag.

If a tagged service is still down after a month, please move it (along with the DOWN tag) to the list of dead hidden services.

The general idea of the remaining four service states below is that, if the Hidden Service Descriptor is available, and something is responding behind it… the service is considered up, and we track that fact on the Main Page. If any of these subsequently go offline, append the DOWN tag and handle as above.

Hello world's / statements, minimal sites, services with low user activity, etc (while boring)… are listed as usual.

Broken services are those that display 404 (and do not use a known hosting service), PHP or other errors (or they fail silently)… any of which prevent the use of the service as intended. They also include blank pages, empty dirs and neglected status notes. Presumably the operator is in limbo. Broken services are tagged with ' (reason) – Broken YYYY-MM-DD' (your guess as to when it went broken)

Services that automatically redirect to another service (such as by HTTP protocol or script) have their redirection destinations noted in their descriptions. These are tagged with ' – Redir YYYY-MM-DD' (your guess as to when it went redir)
Sites that are formally closed via announcement are tagged with ' – Closed YYYY-MM-DD' (your guess as to when it went closed)

Index of pictures

www.ingramcontent.com/pod-product-compliance
Lightning Source LLC
Chambersburg PA
CBHW071412050326
40689CB00010B/1842